CHRISTIANITY
MATTERS

IN THESE
TROUBLED
TIMES

EDITED BY DR KEVIN DONNELLY

Published by:
Wilkinson Publishing Pty Ltd
ACN 006 042 173

PO Box 24135, Melbourne, Victoria, Australia 3001
Ph: 03 9654 5446
www.wilkinsonpublishing.com.au
enquiries@wilkinsonpublishing.com.au

A catalogue record for this book is available from the National Library of Australia

ISBN(s):9781925927894: Paperback

Design by Spike Creative Pty Ltd
Ph: (03) 9427 9500
spikecreative.com.au

Printed and bound in Australia by by Ligare Pty Ltd.

WilkinsonPublishing
wilkinsonpublishinghouse
WPBooks

If Christianity goes, the whole of our culture goes... To our Christian heritage we owe many things beside religious faith. Through it we trace the evolution of our arts, through it we have our conception of Roman Law which has done so much to shape the Western world, through it we have conceptions of public and private morality. And through it we have our common standards of literature, in the literature of Greece and Rome. The Western world has its unity in this heritage, in Christianity and in the ancient civilisations of Greece, Rome and Israel, from which, owing to two thousand years of Christianity, we trace our descent.

– **T.S. Eliot**, *Notes Towards the Definition of Culture*

ACKNOWLEDGEMENTS

This anthology is the second I have edited in what is becoming a series detailing and analysing significant issues and debates impacting on Western societies like Australia. The first book released in 2021 and titled *Cancel Culture and the Left's Long March* is also published by Wilkinson Publishing. While the first anthology deals with the origins and dangers of neo-Marxist inspired political correctness and cancel culture, this anthology deals with Christianity as one of the central foundations of Western civilisation.

Once again, thanks must be given to Kristian Jenkins, John Anderson and the Board of the Page Research Centre who all readily supported this anthology from conception to publication. Those who financially supported the book's publication should also be thanked as well as Michael Wilkinson and Jess Lomas from Wilkinson Publishing.

The relevance and success of *Christianity Matters In These Troubled Times* depends on the research, analysis and exposition carried out by the various authors involved and, as the editor, I would like to thank them for their insightful and valuable contributions. The various authors are experts in their respective fields and represent various Christian denominations.

At a time when Western societies are undergoing epochal challenges and threats represented by what the Italian writer Augusto Del Noce describes as radical secularism, scientism and eroticism this anthology is timely and much needed.

Dr Kevin Donnelly AM

CONTENTS

FOREWORD

Leading historians argue that what should have been no more than a series of ugly border skirmishes turned into the horror of global war in the 1940s largely because Germany and Japan believed that Britain and America, in particular, had grown soft and weak and lost the will to defend democratic freedom.

One straw in the wind in Europe was the famous 'Oxford Pledge' that arose out of the Oxford Union debate in early 1933, where the motion 'this House will never under any circumstances fight for its King and Country' was agreed by 275 votes for the motion and 153 against. The ensuing public uproar could only have sent the message younger British people doubted the value of their culture and did not see it as worth defending, and that the nation was divided.

Churchill, the greatest defender of freedom in the twentieth century, saw what was happening all too clearly. In the same year as the debate he wrote that any society which failed to pass on its story to its children, and in particular that of its religious beliefs and its heroes, was in effect saying to its young their culture was of no value. This left them without purpose, meaning, and direction in life, and open to Karl Marx's dictum that a people deprived of their history are easily persuaded.

It is surely a similar perspective that encouraged Australia's Federal Education Minister, Alan Tudge, to warn our children are being taught to so disapprove of their cultural inheritance that they may not be prepared to defend it.

Worryingly, he may be right. A terrible lack of understanding history, after decades of poor or revisionist or simply no teaching in this area has created a very real void in our understanding of our past – good and bad – that has resulted in the very outcome Churchill warned of and Marx openly advocated. Anxiety, depression and self-harm run at unprecedented levels among young people in our culture, and it is quite apparent that all too often they are also unable to discern reality from ideology in an age when as Thomas Sowell has so acutely pointed out, little Johnny thinks feeling is thinking.

They then find it very difficult not to fall for all sorts of nonsense, including Critical Theory, which is best known for the concept of Critical Race Theory and its insistence that only whites and all whites are racist. As Steven Pinker warns this wokery has spilled out of academia and is now inundating our society despite what he calls its 'surprisingly shallow intellectual roots'.

Frank Ferudi wrote in 2021 of the ideology that is flowing rapidly into the intellectual void that we now see all around us in the crusade to demonise the past by constantly portraying it as a source of 'eternal shame', to the point where 'young people, who know little about the subject, could easily feel ashamed about the nightmarish society into which they were born'.

He cited the constant claims of our 'brutal colonial history' and made the point that though the target of the attacks appears to be our history, the real purpose is to delegitimise the nation we now live in. And why would young people want to defend such a terrible society?

In fact, the story of our settlement is far more nuanced than our children are being taught. Truly understood, there is a wealth of valuable knowledge of both good and bad, noble and inglorious, that can be gleaned from a proper understanding of the era in which Australia was founded.

It was the age of both the Enlightenment and Evangelical reforms, and there was enormous ferment over how best to secure the maximum possible freedoms consistent with protecting the individual against the dangers of mob rule.

More than that, NSW was settled under clear instructions that no slaves were to be kept in the new colony. Why? Because the superpower of the day, England, was in the throes of ending slavery, under the courageous and brilliant Christian activist William Wilberforce and his supporters. No other culture had ever sought to end slavery – including the Indigenous African war-lords who so cruelly captured weaker tribes in order to sell members of their own race to white traders. This is a ground-breaking era in history and yet no quarter is given in the determination of modern-day activists and school curriculum setters to obscure the extraordinary fact it was 'privileged white Christian men and women' who first saw that as, Menzies put it, 'all souls are equal in the eyes of heaven'.

Menzies saw the genius behind democratic freedom is the notion that a higher authority insists that we respect the worth and dignity of all, since left to our devices as history shows we will always clamber over those we regard as somehow lessor. One might ask how the hyper-polarisation and mercilessly unforgiving nature of the identity politics we are increasingly adopting could possibly be a better way for us to create a society in which we enjoy harmony and the opportunity to flourish. As GK Chesterton had it, the 'Good Book' presents a radically different approach, in which we are called to love our neighbours and our enemies even while recognising that often they are one and the same. How blinkered of us to fail to explain that better way of living to our children, so that they might have the opportunity to gain wisdom and understanding and to adopt better ways.

It is all too easy to argue no society should ever have kept slaves, or colonised a land occupied by others, with the benefit of comfortable hindsight. Yet therein lies a vitally important understanding: it is the democracies which have best accommodated change without violence, especially as, bit by often-laborious bit, the full implications of 'loving our neighbour' have permeated our consciousness.

That raises another fascinating reality that it seems very few people care to acknowledge, let alone debate.

It is a fascinating reality that of the 180 or so countries in the world, around 40 have deeply Christian roots. A couple more – Singapore, Japan, Taiwan – have been deeply influenced by Christianity. How, we might ask, are our children ever supposed to understand the world in which they live if something as profoundly interesting and important as this is not at least put before them to ponder? How do we ever expect our children to understand other cultures and other political systems if they are not given any substantive instruction in their own first?

In pulling together this important and thoughtful book, Kevin Donnelly has yet again done us a great service. I hope it is widely read, and that it gets more than a few of our young to start to think deeply and substantially, because our freedoms are like eyesight: once it is lost it is too late to recover.

John Anderson
Chairman of the Page Research Centre and former Deputy Prime Minister of Australia

INTRODUCTION

KRISTIAN JENKINS

Consequently, just as one trespass resulted in condemnation for all people, *so also one righteous act resulted in justification for* all people. Romans 5:18

This scandalous claim was made by the Apostle Paul in his letter to the Christian community in Rome around 55AD, not much more than 20 years after the death and resurrection of Jesus Christ, whose righteous act he is referring to. This phrase, like so many in the Bible, is fraught with theological complexity, and its proper meaning is still debated today, but what is clear is that whatever is being offered here is available to *all people.* Not only to the nation of Israel, God's chosen people; not only to kings and rulers; not only to those possessing special knowledge; not even only to certain moral or holy people – no, this promise is available to *all people.* Women as well as men; Gentiles as well as Jews; slaves as well as masters.

For God so loved the world that he gave his one and only Son, that whoever believes in him shall not perish but have eternal life. John 3:16

God's love is for the whole *world*, and *whoever* will come and partake of it is welcome. Because we are all made in the image of God and are beloved by God, we are all imbued with infinite dignity and worth.

The universalism of the Christian call was perhaps the most scandalous and revolutionary aspect of it to the ancient world; to Jews, who believed God's calling was especially for them, and to Greeks, whose society was ordered by rigid hierarchies, where the poor and dispossessed in particular could forget any hope of divine love and mercy. Even today, many socio-religious cultures would consider the notion of the inherent dignity and worth of *every* person absurd. Not so in the democratic West, however, where every individual is sacralised and where the notion of universal human rights is considered an irrefutable cardinal doctrine. Larry Siedentop's *Inventing the Individual, The Origins of Western Liberalism*, details how Christ's teachings represented a revolutionary message that underpins and enriches the liberties and freedoms we now take for granted.

What accounts for this? The answer should be obvious. Christ, Paul and the other founders of Christianity are the progenitors of this idea, and the Christian West, beginning in Europe, then later spreading across the globe through European imperialism, including to Australia, was the first and greatest beneficiary of this idea. It is only because Western civilisation as we experience it today was formed by two millennia of Christian catechesis, that everyone believes everyone is worthy of dignity and respect. It's also why everyone believes in one person, one vote; equality for all before the law; that slavery is wrong; that women are equal to men; that the sick and the poor should be afforded care; even that every child should be given an education, an idea that grew out of the Protestant reformation on the grounds that each person should be able to read and understand the Word of God for themselves.

Many in the West today are ignorant of these facts, and some outright refute them. The historical irony is that today we hear preached the lie that patriarchal Christian imperialism, as it's fashioned, is the greatest enemy to human equality in history. This is simply not true. Were it not for the teachings of Christ and his followers there would be no separation of church and state, no individual liberty, no universal health and education, no Enlightenment, no abolition of slavery, no feminism, no civil rights movement, and perhaps worst of all, no Christmas. Even ideas which explicitly deny Christian truth like communism, materialism and even atheism could only have grown out of the Christian West.

This is the thesis of *Dominion*, by Tom Holland, a lapsed Anglican who by his own admission no longer believes in God. He says:

> *Assumptions that I had grown up with – about how a society should be properly organised, and the principles that it should uphold – were not bred of classical antiquity, still less of 'human nature,' but very distinctively of that civilisation's Christian past. So profound has been the impact of Christianity on the development of Western civilisation that it has come to be hidden from view.*

This is the thesis of this anthology as well, because this is a truth that is not only increasingly forgotten, but also widely and falsely refuted, and it is a truth that must be restated for each generation. It is no historical accident that the freest, wealthiest and most peaceful societies in human history are the fruits of a Christian civilisation, and if we want to continue to enjoy those fruits then the efforts to cut them away from the vine that supports them ought to be challenged.

This volume brings together some of the finest Christian thinkers and writers in Australia today in order to raise this challenge anew. We will hear from Cardinal Pell on how the spiritual and transcendent aspirations of Christianity have given flight to the vitality of our collective cultural soul. Stuart Piggin shows how Christian the foundations of modern Australia actually are. Peter Craven reminds us of how anaemic and listless Western art, literature and music might have been if it had not been animated by the Spirit of Christ as it has been. We will remember the Christian foundations of education, the University, the health and social welfare systems and our political and legal systems. As detailed by Wanda Skowronska, Christianity is especially under attack in the West today, but there is always a way forward, and Martyn Iles shows us how the Christian citizen can lead in that direction, as those committed to Christ's teachings have done in the past. Importantly, Peter Rosengren's chapter

acknowledges the sins committed in the name of Christianity and Tess
Livingstone details the flaws and challenges faced by the Church of Rome.

Christ came that we might have life, and have it to the full (John 10:10),
and in the West we have been the blessed recipients of this precious
inheritance. But it is an inheritance that is slipping away as we wilfully
cut ourselves off from our Christian roots. May this anthology be another
clarion call to cling to that which has brought us so much good, the holy
Gospel of Jesus Christ our Lord and Saviour.

First Australians and Australia First: The Story of Maria Yellomundee

Stuart Piggin

Every year as I join my fellow academics at graduation ceremonies at Macquarie University, I am told by the young First Australian who leads us in the recognition of country that he is a proud descendent of Maria Yellomundee. Who was she? It's a great story, actually, of one who stayed afloat, though tossed about in the eddies and whirlpools of currents still running strongly in Australian history. Is it possible to recover now from existing sources what really happened? Is it yesterday's pro-European perspective in those sources which makes the history of Aboriginal encounter with Europeans so hard to tell? Or is it rather today's anti-colonial perspective on that encounter which makes the history so hard to hear?

What credence can be given to the claim of James Stephen, undersecretary in the Colonial Office, that Britain, by imparting 'her religion, her laws, her language, her literature, and her civil franchises' to the Australian colonies, gave as beneficent a demonstration of the 'art of colonisation' as the world has experienced? Or, are we dealing here, as one commentator has written, with 'origins that cannot be contemplated without horror'?

Maria's story is an opportunity to navigate a path between the two extremes. Applicable to the most pressing and least resolved issue in our national history, it is a story of those on both sides of a vast divide who together achieved small successes against the odds and began to lay the foundation of a reconciled community still to be built. The voice of Christian humanitarianism, a force for amelioration in racial conflict in Australia's past, must continue to be heard in the conversation if the health of our nation is to be realised.

The difficulty of understanding the history of this encounter reaches beyond biased sources and impassioned perspectives to the complexity of the encounter itself. Governors vacillated between kindly indulgence and harsh repression, uncertain how or if English law applied to indigenous peoples's actions in any conflicts. There was no simple racial divide: some Aborigines joined settler communities, sharing access to food and water, while there were whites (normally convicts) who sided with Aborigines in raiding settlers' farms. Aborigines joined soldiers' and settlers' search parties, while some whites protected Aborigines to evade capture. Some Aborigines were considered 'wild', while others were believed to be 'domesticated', but settlers were not always agreed on which was which, sometimes betraying those who had been loyal to them, and sometimes betrayed by those they thought they could trust.

This unstable and unpromising chaos demanded a better way. A Christian missionary (William Shelley) and a Christian governor (Lachlan Macquarie) between them devised a plan to deliver a long-term solution: first Christianise and educate Aboriginal children, then marry them to partners who had undergone the same 'civilising' process, and then settle them on small farms given as land grants by the governor. Maria Yellomundee was destined to be the first Aborigine to be enlisted in the plan. Demonstrably, she not only survived, but thrived, becoming, historian Grace Karskens tells us, 'the matriarch of a vast family, and her

descendants now number in their thousands' (*The Colony*, 2010, 450).
How is this gratifying outcome to be explained?

Maria was born, about 1805, north-west of Sydney on the flood plain
of the fast-flowing Hawkesbury River at Richmond Bottoms (Lowlands
today!). Her Darug name was Bolongaia. Flowing into the Hawkesbury
(known as Deerubbin by the Darug) from the west is the Grose River, and
the Grose and Hawkesbury at their confluence are joined by a third river
running from the south, the Nepean. It is better understood as one river,
the Nepean/Hawkesbury, and it arcs around Sydney in a great semi-circle.
It regularly inundated much of Western Sydney in flood and abandoned it
in drought, so that European settlers were propelled ever further inland in
search of higher ground and supplementary pasture. In the process, they
displaced the First Australians, the Darug of what is now Western Sydney
and the Gandangara of the Southern Highlands. The European settlers
had been instructed to 'conciliate' the 'affections' of the 'Natives' and 'to
live in amity and kindness with them'. In a pattern eventually repeated all
over the continent, relations between 'Natives' and Europeans often began
with mutual goodwill, quickly followed by conflict and killings, and ended
with the establishment of an institution or mission of which the Native
Institution at Parramatta, attended by Maria, was the prototype.

Maria was the daughter of Yellomundee (Yarramundi), an elder of
the Boorooberongal clan of the Darug nation, born about 1760, and
granddaughter of Gombeeree, born in the 1740s. Both men had two
wives, but it is not known who Maria's mother was. Both were karadji,
that is, doctors of renown. It is of significance to our story that the first
Europeans they encountered were sensitive to the plight of indigenous
people. On 14 April 1791 Yellomundee and Gombeeree were introduced
to a party of Europeans engaged in exploring the land west of Parramatta.
Along with Governor Phillip, it was headed by marine officers William
Dawes and Watkin Tench, both men of conscience, well-educated,

representatives, we may say, of revelation and reason respectively. Dawes was a devout Christian and had already made a study of the language of the Eora peoples around Sydney.

Tench, like Governor Phillip, had imbibed Enlightenment ideas, but in his popular account of his adventures in the new settlement, he extensively quoted from Milton's *Paradise Lost* in evocation of the feelings he experienced in this strange new land. Two years earlier, on leading a similar party west of Parramatta, Tench, on reaching Prospect Hill, recalled Milton's depiction of Satan, looking 'on the wild Abyss... pondering his voyage'. He was sensitive to the ambiguity brought by the newcomers: he found the landscape wild and threatening, but both he and Dawes were mindful that they were themselves threatening to its inhabitants. Though ultimately powerless to protect the Aborigines, such awareness enabled Tench and Dawes to question policies or practices of their superiors which disadvantaged Aborigines.

Their initial meeting with Yellomundee was congenial. He welcomed them to his country on the Cumberland Plain and may then have discerned that negotiating with some of the newcomers was both possible and wise. For their part, Europeans, in need of authority figures with whom to negotiate, identified him as the chief, even king, of the Richmond tribe. In 1803 Samuel Marsden, chaplain and magistrate, relied on Yellomundee to bring hostilities on the Hawkesbury to a conclusion.

On 28 December 1814 in Parramatta Governor Macquarie presided at an inaugural conference and feast to be held annually for Aborigines. Yellomundee and other members of his clan, including Maria, were among those who attended. Following a conversation with Macquarie, Yellomundee placed Maria in the care of William and Elizabeth Shelley, founders of the Native Institution. Shelley, who had served as a missionary with the London Missionary Society in Tonga, first suggested the Institution a year earlier, apparently in response to a successful move by William Wilberforce in 1813 to change the charter of the East India Company to require it to fund hospitals and schools in India. The ameliorative impact of Christian humanitarianism began to be felt throughout the Empire.

By mid-1814 Macquarie had become open to the Shelleys' proposal because the relationship between Aboriginal people and white settlers was then particularly perilous. It was in the middle of a drought. The Aborigines were hungry and their traditional food sources had been destroyed, and being gatherers as well as hunters, helped themselves to the settlers' crops. Near Appin, south of Campbelltown, Aborigines were murdered, including women and children. They were buried on a farm owned by John Kennedy. He was long known for his sympathy for Aboriginal people. Over a decade earlier (1805) he had assisted Aboriginal women to broker an agreement between Marsden and Aborigines of the Cowpastures and Prospect areas to hold a conference 'with a view to opening the way to reconciliation'. Now he arranged for the murdered Aborigines to be buried on his farm in properly fenced-off graves even though they were not murdered there.

This was considered a humane act at the time. Then, following a massacre in 1816 at Appin, now commemorated annually, he protected from arrest some Aborigines, proscribed by Macquarie, insisting on their innocence and that, if they were arrested, he would have to 'abandon the country'. What motivated him in his enduring support for Aborigines?

Next to Kennedy's farm is Humewood farm named after Andrew Hume and his wife, Eliza, who was Kennedy's aunt. She had arrived in NSW in 1795 and had been the first matron of the Female Orphanage started by Anne, wife of Governor King, in 1801. Eliza's son Hamilton Hume was the famous explorer, revered like John Kennedy for his concern for First Australians.

This is where the story gets really interesting, connecting Maria with the most powerful of spiritual and humanitarian developments in Britain. Eliza, Kennedy's aunt and Hamilton's mother, was the daughter of the Revd John Kennedy, Vicar of Teston, a town in Kent, England. In Appin, NSW, Kennedy's farm was known as Teston farm. The Revd John Kennedy became vicar of Teston, Kent, in 1789 in succession to the Revd James Ramsay who is revered in the anti-slavery movement as *the* pioneer abolitionist.

A monument to Ramsay at the Church of St Peter and St Paul, Teston, testifies to his 'tender attention to each social duty, benevolence to the whole human race… of whatever clime or colony'. It was an attention which reached the colony of NSW and the Aboriginal race. Ramsay brought together pioneers of the movement for the abolition of slavery, including his patron, Charles Middleton and his wife, Margaret, Samuel Johnson, compiler of the English dictionary, William Wilberforce who was to become the most famous of the campaigners against the slave trade, and Hannah More, champion of the education of the poor.

This group, which has been labelled the Teston Set or Network, preceded and anticipated the work of the more famous reformist 'Clapham Sect', over which Wilberforce was to preside. Charles Middleton lived in Barham Court in Teston, the ancestral home of the Gambiers, a Huguenot family. His wife, Margaret Gambier, had been converted to 'vital faith' through George Whitefield in the Evangelical Revival and appears to have made membership of the group a delightful pleasure as well as a high calling and duty.

It was Charles Middleton, Comptroller of the British Navy, who was chiefly responsible for the success of the first fleet. He ensured the lot of convicts in the voyage would be nothing like the experience of the slave trade that he was determined to eliminate. Middleton chose the eleven ships of the first fleet with great attention to their seaworthiness. He had them so well provisioned that the convicts alighted in Sydney Cove heavier than when they boarded in Portsmouth 262 days before. The first fleet was one of the greatest maritime achievements of the age. It was extraordinary that all eleven vessels arrived safely, after the 16,000-mile voyage, with hardly any loss of life. The Teston Set, then, ameliorated the sufferings of convicts, and now, through the Kennedys and Humes and the opening of the Native Institution, it was involved in addressing the plight of those who stood to suffer far more, the First Australians.

Maria's name was the first on a list of all 37 of the Aboriginal children enrolled in the Native Institution in Parramatta between 1814 and 1820. The list was compiled by the Revd Richard Hill. He arrived in 1819 and was the principal founder of the NSW Society for Promoting Christian Knowledge Among the Aborigines. Hill noted of Maria that she 'Spells four syllables in the Bible and reads'. Whatever that means, it suggests she was ahead of the other children in her 'state of learning'.

It is commonly claimed today that the 'stolen generations' practice commenced with the Native Institution's child acquisition policies. The evidence is inconclusive. Maria was placed there voluntarily by her father, Yellomundee. But in 1818, the Methodist minister, Walter Lawry, was informed by Yellomundee himself that women and children ran away from him because 'men in black clothes' had previously taken away their children to put them in the Native Institution. Macquarie claimed that the last intake of five Aboriginal children 'were of their own accord sent into the Institution by their parents' (J. Brooks and J.L. Kohen, *The Parramatta Native Institution and the Black Town*, University of New South Wales Press, 1991, 82, 263).

It was obviously important to Macquarie to argue that the children were not compelled to enter the Institution, let alone 'stolen'. Yet there is no doubt that Shelley had planned the Institution so that the children would be educated apart from their parents. Nor is there any evidence that European settlers at the time dissented from the view that only by educating the children apart from their parents was there any hope of 'civilising' them. This attitude made the European project of 'civilising' the original inhabitants of the land very difficult despite the best intentions of those with humanitarian and Christian impulses.

There is evidence, however, that some Aboriginal parents were delighted by the progress their children in the Native Institution made in the acquisition of the elements of European culture. In spite of all the obstacles, then, the contribution of the Native Institution to equipping Aborigines to survive in this new world is begrudgingly conceded by fair-minded historians, even those with little sympathy for the aspirations of missionaries:

> On the face of it, the Institution was hardly a success, but if those 'lucky' enough to have gained an education passed their acquired knowledge on to their children, the benefits gained at the Institution would flow on. Unknowingly, the ex-students would be the purveyors of education, and to some degree had become social workers to their people… Like it or not… they were assimilated, and even if they were not absorbed into their invaders' lifestyle, they could now handle the culture shock marginally better than many of their forlorn race.
> (Brooks and Kohen, *The Parramatta Native Institution*, 88).

In 1819 Maria, in her fourth and final year in the Native Institution, stunned the colony by taking the first prize in the public examinations, defeating almost 100 white children in the process. The missionaries were thrilled. Maria's achievement vindicated the evangelical Christian belief in the equality of all races and both sexes in intellect. Robert Howe, printer and editor of the *Sydney Gazette,* who became a Methodist that same year following conversion to vital religion, enthused of Maria's achievement that 'we have already the happiness of contemplating in the infant bud the richness of the expanding flower'.

Especially gratified by Maria's success was Elizabeth Shelley who bore the burden of teaching and caring for the children in the Native Institution during its years at Parramatta (1814-22). She had four sons and three daughters of her own with William. But in the first year of the Institution's operation, William died. Elizabeth never remarried and outlived her husband by 63 years. She continued to visit her former pupils after they were moved from Parramatta to Black Town (now Blacktown). She gave them what was needed, but few provided, namely unbroken care and concern over decades.

The Shelleys had been realistic enough to accept that it would be difficult for even educated Aboriginal girls to find a similarly-educated white marriage partner, so they suggested that they might settle for an Aboriginal man or a convict, providing they had good morals and faith in Christ. Very paternalistic, you think. But Maria ran with the suggestion – she may have settled for both!

In 1822, Maria was being 'maternally treated' in the household of Shelley's newly-married missionary friends, Thomas and Ann Hassall. Thomas was the son of Rowland Hassall, also a missionary who arrived in NSW in 1798. Ann was the eldest daughter of the Revd Samuel Marsden. She had been sent back to England for her education when she was six. Her parents had taken in at least two native boys and her mother taught them how to read, an adumbration of the Native Institution. Ann's separation from her own parents and her familiarity with their largely unsuccessful attempts to educate Aboriginal children would have sensitised her to Maria's experience.

Thomas opened the first Sunday School in Australia in 1813. By 1817 it had 25 teachers and 150 pupils. It was attended by children from the Native Institution, who made 'very rapid progress', as well as white children. Ann was a teacher in the school before she married Thomas. She probably knew Maria very well and was evidently sufficiently impressed by her to offer her a position in her own household.

In the same year as Thomas and Ann Hassall were married (1822), Maria herself may have married an Aborigine called 'Dickey'. The evidence is inconclusive as both 'Maria' and 'Dickey' were names commonly given to Aborigines by Europeans. The famous Bennelong had a son called 'Dickey'. He was baptised Thomas Walker Coke, named after John Wesley's successor and a founder of the Wesleyan Methodist Missionary Society. Dickey, who may have attended the Native Institution, was then living with another missionary, the Wesleyan William Walker who was the first missionary appointed exclusively to work among the Aborigines. They thought of him as 'their parson'.

On 8 September 1822, with great joy, he baptised Dickey, the first Aborigine to be baptised, and, historian John Harris tells us, the first Aboriginal evangelist. Dickey was the son of Bennelong's third wife, Boorong. She had lived for about 18 months in 1789–90 with the first chaplain, Richard Johnson, and his wife Mary. In October 1790, she returned to her own people apparently unconverted to Christianity. But she did give birth to Dickey who became a Christian evangelist, as we have seen, and it may have been he who married Maria in 1822. He was certainly the sort of Christianised, Europeanised Aborigine the missionaries would have been happy for Maria to marry. But Dickey died in early 1823 and is buried alongside the missionaries themselves in St John's Cemetery, Parramatta. Walker grieved deeply over Dickey's death and on 14 May married Eliza Hassall, of whom Walker observed, 'next to real piety, is her attachment to the poor blacks'.

Then, on the 36th anniversary of the settlement of the colony (26 January 1824) in St John's Parramatta, Maria married Robert Lock, a convict carpenter working on the building of the new Native Institution, now relocated from Parramatta to Black Town. Maria and Robert were both given employment by the Revd Robert Cartwright. Having arrived in Sydney in 1810, Cartwright was appointed chaplain to the Hawkesbury settlement at Windsor. He was clear about what he wanted to achieve and why, but not yet how:

> The great Creator having made of One Blood all Nations of the Earth, and taking for granted that the Natives of New South Wales are capable of instruction and civilization... what plan can be adopted, what means used, or what steps taken, whereby we may most speedily and effectually civilize and evangelize the Natives of New South Wales, local circumstances considered?
>
> (*Sydney Gazette,* 14 July 1810).

Macquarie, as part of his response to the 1816 uprising and with Cartwright's encouragement, made land grants to compliant Aborigines in the area which became Blacktown. These included four-acre farms, and Maria and Robert Lock first lived on one of these following their marriage in 1824. Because Robert was only three years through his seven-year sentence, he was assigned to Maria, and she was promised a grant of land and a cow as 'a marriage portion'. In 1825 Maria and Robert moved to Liverpool where they worked on Cartwright's farm, Robert erecting farm buildings there.

By 1831 Maria had received the cow, but still not her land grant, and in that year she petitioned Governor Darling for the promise to be honoured through the granting of thirty acres at Black Town. She identified herself in the petition as 'an Aboriginal Native of New South Wales', the daughter of 'the Chief of the Richmond Tribes'. At the bottom of the petition, which was written in copperplate, is Cartwright's scribbled addendum:

> I beg leave to state for the information of His Excellency the Governor, that I have known the Petitioner from a child – but more particularly since she was married – having in consequence of her exemplary conduct allowed her and her husband, for several years past, to reside upon my farm. I believe her own written statement to be strictly correct and I feel great pleasure in recommending Petitioner to His Excellency's most favourable consideration.

It appears that all the clergy spoke well of Maria. The Revd Richard Hill, Secretary of the Native Institution, observed that she 'has proved that the instructions she received was not lost upon her' and Wesleyan missionary William Walker joined Cartwright in commending her to the Governor's 'kind consideration'.

Darling was persuaded and decreed that land be allotted to the Locks, but it was to be as close as possible to Cartwright's farm at Liverpool rather than at Black Town. When the chaplain discovered that the proposed grant would cut through his farm buildings, ironically those which Lock had built, he withdrew his support, asking that the Locks be granted land at Black Town instead, claiming that Maria wished to return to Black Town anyway.

Finally, in 1833, Maria was granted 40 acres at Liverpool. A decade later, she relocated to Black Town, having successfully applied for 30 acres there, soon to be supplemented by a further 30 acres. The last of her ten children was born there in 1844. Nine of her children survived her. Robert died in 1854, and Maria in 1878. She was buried beside Robert at St Bartholomew's Church of England, Prospect. She was at her death the owner of 40 acres in Liverpool and 60 in Blacktown. It does appear that between them the Cartwrights and Locks did achieve a tangible benefit. It was at Blacktown that Cartwright as early as 1816 had planned to establish an Aboriginal settlement and seminary which would be distant from European contamination, an idea which became integral to Aboriginal missions for the next half century.

Those missions chronically failed, but Blacktown was to become the most successful Aboriginal/European settlement in Australian history. It helped that the Aboriginal families who continued to live in Blacktown were those with traditional links to the region and were therefore living on their own tribal lands. In 1874 a public school was opened at Rooty Hill to cater for the descendants of the nearby Black Town Native

Institution, including at least ten of Maria's grandchildren. The opening
was assessed as 'historically important' because 'it continued the unbroken
link between Aboriginal occupation and education that had been firmly
established in the area' (Brooks and Kohen, *The Parramatta Native
Institution,* 240, 267).

Maria's story is remarkable for two major reasons. First, it involved an
astonishing number of departures from social conventions.

- A black married to a white
- A man assigned to a woman
- A white man assigned to an indigenous woman
- A woman was allowed to acquire property in her own name
- An indigenous woman was allowed to acquire property in her
  own name.

Such was the length early NSW society was prepared to go, in this
case, in support of marriage and stable family life. That family stability
is foundational to local community and national stability is one of those
beliefs not as strongly endorsed today as it was in Maria's time.

A second remarkable feature of Maria's story is that it mobilised a small
army of Christian workers who laboured to make the Native Institution
a successful experiment in preparing Aborigines to adjust to Western
culture. Among the Christian families who supported Maria were the
Shelleys, Kennedys, Marsdens, Hassalls, Cartwrights, and Walkers,
dynasties still active today in Christian work. They were all involved in
helping to make Maria Yellomundee the person she was and in making
her own family the dynasty it has become.

Academic historians look rather to matters of race, gender and class to
explain how history is made, but family dynasties, in which women were
often the principal players, Christian reformist fellowships such as the
Clapham and Teston networks, and Christian humanitarian values may
be of equal importance in explaining our personal and public historical

experiences. The story of Maria Yellomundee is 'arguably the ultimate success story of Governor Macquarie's experiment to blend two disparate cultures' (Brooks and Kohen, *The Parramatta Native Institution*, 248). It is a story worth telling and, even more, worth hearing if we are to preserve from the past insights most propitious to our national future.

Designated 'the historian of the Australian soul', Stuart Piggin has co-authored the prize-winning two-volume history of Australian Evangelical Christians, The Fountain of Public Prosperity *(2018) and* Attending to the National Soul *(2020). Acclaimed a 'masterwork', they are 'the fullest account' of the impact of Christianity on Australian history. In his capacity as Director of the Centre for the History of Christian Thought and Experience at Macquarie University from 2005 to 2016, he supervised 28 doctoral candidates, working principally on areas of Australian religious history and on the application of Classical and Christian thought to the modern world. The founding president of the Evangelical History Association of Australia, he is a committed Evangelical Anglican, with a special interest in Jonathan Edwards, the Church's foremost theologian of Revival, and the history of missions. He has also written major studies of the Australian experience of community disasters.*

GOD: HOME ALONE IN AUSTRALIA?

Cardinal George Pell

> *God, you are my God, I pine for you;*
> *my heart thirsts for you,*
> *my body longs for you,*
> *as a land parched, dreary and waterless.*
> *Thus I have gazed on you in the sanctuary.*
> *seeing your power and your glory.*

These beautiful lines from Psalm 63 make up part of the official daily prayer of the Church prescribed for clergy and religious. They are a reminder, a call to recollection and self-examination and at different times over the years of my priestly life, mainly in Australia, I wondered whether the lines accurately fitted my state of soul and mind. How many Australians would choose to recite this prayer for themselves?

I am more used to the version from the breviary which runs:

> *My body pines for you (God)*
> *like a dry, weary land without water.*

Most parts of Australia are often short of rain and all Australians know about drought. This is imagery that we completely understand, but nobody would claim that Australia as a collectivity could be described as searching and longing for God in this way.

When I was recently on an enforced secular retreat for 404 days as a guest of Her Majesty, I received around 4,000 letters from countries around the world. Many came from Australia and one of these was written by a priest friend with a country parish and a very small number of worshippers in his couple of churches. He explained that he did not know anyone in his area with this thirst for God. Naturally he was an exception to his own rule, but it was a disconcerting claim even for a tiny congregation. In many parishes in Melbourne and in Sydney (in my experience), the congregations at daily Mass were as large as they have ever been in living memory, despite the drop in the numbers of Sunday Mass. A number of these parishioners were elderly, perhaps grandparents praying for their grandchildren who had drifted away from practice and belief, but nearly everywhere across the vast national network of parishes we find a faithful remnant of worshippers and believers, often substantial remnants.

The tides of unbelief are running strongly in Australian society, as the Christian majority of 52%, including the Catholic community of 22%, are outgunned by the forces of 'the world, the flesh and the devil'. Evil in its many forms can be fascinating, and our understated beliefs do not always provide the best defence.

A couple of straws in the wind are not misleading. In stark contrast to public life in the United States, God is rarely mentioned by politicians in Australia in their public utterances. I can think of only one spectacular exception across fifty years and he was a state premier accused of corruption.

When I was Archbishop of Melbourne, Catholic secondary schools would send me copies of the annual school magazines. During one Christmas break, I leafed through about fifteen of these to read their accounts of their annual student retreats. In those days, nearly every school had a retreat of a few days for all their senior secondary students that were duly recorded. However, in the overwhelmingly sympathetic reports on these gatherings, generally written by a student, I found only a

GOD: HOME ALONE IN AUSTRALIA?

few references to God; and not many more to Christ. I do not doubt that each group prayed and that the Mass was celebrated for them, but the silence about God raised a question mark for me. We are tempted to take God for granted, like a well-loved but distant grandfather, or, even worse, as a comforting background noise.

Monotheists

Catholics, like all Christians, are monotheists who believe in the one true God, Creator of heaven and earth; of our small miraculous world, unique in its intelligent life, in the unfathomable mysteries and the immeasurable expanse of our dark, cold universe. Christians are children of the Jewish tradition and believe in the God of Abraham, Isaac, and Jacob, who is the Father of Our Lord Jesus Christ.

Christians can admire God's handiwork in his creation, in the power of the ocean, the extent of the deserts, the beauty of the daily sunrise. But these are reflections of God's creativity, they are not part of God, not immediate parts of his nature.

In the Jewish scriptures, the Old Testament God was known as El or Elohim, as the Jews acknowledged the numinous, moved beyond polytheism, shared to some degree the traditions of the Phoenicians and the Canaanites about the one God, and then God revealed himself to Moses as Yahweh, 'I am whom I am' or 'I am he who is' (Exodus 3:14), the proper name of the God they were worshipping. Christians today belong to a millennial tradition of belief; we benefit from everything that has been revealed to the prophets and the saints.

The Church teaches that this one true God is Spirit; merciful, all-powerful and ever faithful. God is good and wise, neither cruel nor capricious. God is infinite, without beginning and without end, the all-powerful lord of history, who will oversee the final separation of the good from the bad. Unlike the capricious pagan gods of ancient Greece and

Rome, God is interested in us, cares for us, and has told us how to live.

Christians believe the one God is a Trinity of persons, God the Father, the eternal Source; the Son of God, i.e. Jesus Christ, true God and true man, who showed us by his life and by teaching what God is like, and the Holy Spirit, who lives in the hearts of all the faithful.

God is not the most powerful figure in space and time, the cosmic trigger of the Big Bang. God is beyond space and time. He is Being itself, transcendent, incomprehensible.

No explanation is adequate to explain this Mystery. We are told St. Patrick used the three leaves of a shamrock; others have used the three states of water, liquid, ice, steam; still others have compared the Trinity to a family or community, or to a triangle overlaying a circle. What is most important however is to remember that God loves every one of us, keeps each one of us in the palm of his hand. God is an all-embracing torrent of love, spreading forgiveness and kindness to all, especially those who want to be loved.

The Christian literature across 2000 years abounds in pen-pictures of the Transcendent, evocations of the supernatural, the spiritual.

The most spectacular are from the last book in the Christian Bible, the Book of Revelation about the Prelude to the Great Day of the Lord, the coming of the Heavenly Jerusalem, the One sitting on the throne, the Lion of the tribe of Judah, the Root of David, and the Lamb who had been sacrificed and was worthy 'to receive power, riches, wisdom, strength, honour, glory, and blessing' (c. 4). There are the plagues, the mighty conflict between the woman clothed with the sun and the huge, red dragon with seven heads (c. 12), the angels against the false prophets and slaves of the beast.

And the triumph of the 144,000 virgins, companions of the Lamb, creating 'a sound coming out of heaven like the sound of the ocean or the roar of thunder; it was the sound of harpists playing their harps' (c. 14).

The North African St. Augustine (354–430 AD), the finest theologian of the first millennium writes in a different key. He was baptised by St. Ambrose in Milan at the age of thirty-three, after a long moral and intellectual struggle. 'Give me chastity and continence, but not yet' (8:7 Confessions). He believed that God 'made us for yourself and our hearts find no peace until they rest in you' (1.1 Confessions). Many are still ill at ease today, some despairing, but many do not connect their angst to God's absence.

In a famous passage, Augustine described his conversion beautifully. 'I have learnt to love you late. Beauty at once so ancient and so new... I searched for you outside myself, and disfigured as I was, I fell upon the lovely things of your creation... I tasted you, and now I hunger and thirst for you. You touched me, and I am inflamed with love of your peace' (Confessions 10.27).

The Confessions are the first autobiography in Western literature and Augustine writes with a level of insight about himself and the good God, which is worthy of a great novelist such as Evelyn Waugh.

Each of us is destined to encounter the supernatural at the moment of death as Christians do not believe that life ends at death, even for those who are evil.

The nineteenth century English cardinal St. John Henry Newman combined with the composer Edward Elgar to produce the Dream of Gerontius, a masterpiece 'awfully solemn and mystic', in Elgar's words, about such a moment.

Gerontius knows he is near to death, chill at heart, with faltering breath and dampened brow, but he rallies:

> Raise thou my fainting soul and play the man;
> And through such evening span
> of life and thought as still has to be trod,
> Prepare to meet thy God.

The angels are supportive and the devils are repulsed and Gerontius prays the magnificent hymn:

> *Firmly I believe and truly*
> *God is three and God is one*
> *And I next acknowledge duly*
> *Manhood taken by the Son.*

And he affirms that he loves 'supremely, solely Him the Holy, Him the strong'.

And so Gerontius tended and nursed by the angels, accompanied by 'Masses on earth, and prayers in heaven' comes safely to 'the throne of Most Highest'.

So may it be with all of us.

Down To Earth

The basis of the whole Christian religion is Jesus' teaching that the one true God loves each one of us like a loving father. On occasions in the gospels, Our Lord called God 'abba', which is translated as 'father', or more accurately for us as 'dad' because 'abba' was used by children, young or grown-up, talking to their father in the intimacy of the family. He also gave us the parable of the prodigal son; a misleading title because we learn here what God is like. A better title would be the parable of the loving father.

We all know the story from Luke's Gospel (Ch. 15:11-32) of the wild younger son, probably around 17 years of age, who pestered his father for his share of the inheritance, obtained this and then left for the bright lights where he proceeded to waste everything, to blow the lot in riotous living, in debauchery, as the Gospel explains.

A recession also hit the district and in the absence of any social service benefits, the young fellow had to take a job looking after pigs. For Jews, the pig is an unclean animal ('Cursed be the man who breeds swine' says the Talmud). So his situation represents the ultimate degradation. He even had to steal his food to survive.

In this predicament he realised that he would be better off working for his father at home and moving from this somewhat selfish realisation, he confessed that he had wronged his father and sinned against heaven. He decided to travel home and try for a job on the family farm.

His father might have responded in a number of ways, for example explaining that there was no place for him in the family as he had made no contact for years; that his mother had died and this departure had hastened her death. Alternatively, he might have wished the son well and offered him a job on an outlying part of the farm, but explained that things had changed too much for him to return to the family circle.

The father did neither. He ran to the boy and kissed him, gave him a fine robe and a beautiful ring, symbols of honour and authority. He gave him sandals, so that the boy would not be barefoot like a slave. Meat was eaten rarely, but the father ordered the slaughter of the best fatted calf and a huge welcome-home party.

Often there is an unexpected twist in Jesus' parables. Here the older brother returns home from work to find the party in full swing and complains bitterly to his father that this no-hoper who had lost so much family money, spent on girlfriends, was now being given a party, the likes of which he himself had not received for his twenty-first birthday.

We do not know whether the older brother was eventually reconciled, as the father explained he was much appreciated, that the inheritance was his, 'but it was only right we should celebrate and rejoice, because your brother he was dead and has come to life, he was lost and is found'.

In this parable we enter into the heart of God, who is behind the Big Bang, DNA; who endowed the geniuses who discovered these truths; who inspired Mary, Jesus' mother, St. Paul, Mother Teresa, as well as Bach and Beethoven, Dante and Shakespeare, Newton and Einstein, Plato and Aristotle, and the incomparable Michelangelo.

Filling A Gap

During the years between 1987 and 1996 when I was an auxiliary bishop, I celebrated more than 50 confirmations a year, generally of 1500-2000 grade six boys and girls across the Archdiocese of Melbourne. I nearly always succeeded in having a forty-five-minute class with each group, an experience I thoroughly enjoyed (and most of them did also).

Originally, I spoke about the sacrament of Confirmation complementing Baptism, and of the gifts and fruits of the Holy Spirit, but within a few months I made two changes. Instead of giving a lecture, I adopted the methodology Barry Humphries used for his appearances as Dame Edna Everage where of course I followed a narrative line but proceeded by asking questions and relying on their answers to take the conversation forward. In the senior primary and junior secondary years, students will happily answer questions, so I would question them for a half hour or so and then allow them to ask me any questions they chose for ten or so minutes. The format always worked and the mix of questions was predictable, from self-confident Aussie youngsters with different levels of religious understanding and prudence. Once in a while the comments would not have been out of place at a post-graduate theology seminary. In a rich bay-side parish, I once received a line of questions on the financial package I received as archbishop. The celibacy of the clergy and women priests were regular topics.

The second change I made was to direct my questions to the basic elements of the Christian 'Kerygma', the Good News we followed rather than the sacrament itself; on God, Christ, love, prayer, forgiveness, the Church, papacy. Did we need to be sorry (repent) for our sins in order to obtain forgiveness in confession? My alternative scenarios for different penitents always provoked division, but no one objected to the Ten Commandments.

We regularly came to an early consensus on what a Christian is (a theist who believes Christ is God's Son), although some were unsure whether the Anglicans and Protestants qualified; but when I asked what a Catholic was, there was regularly silence. During such a pause one child said, 'We're Catholics, aren't we?' (I agreed), so I often asked during later silences 'You're Catholics, aren't you?' The Catholics all agreed quickly and happily, and then we worked to identify what distinguished us from other theists, such as Jews and Muslims, and other Christians.

Unsurprisingly, the topic of God was baffling, producing long and generally thoughtful silences, when I would provoke them by asking what God was made of: 'sugar and spice and everything nice'. Early on during one profound silence, a cheeky young boy said with a smile that God was 'unreal'. At that period 'unreal' was an adjective youngsters would use to describe an experience or object they really liked and approved of. But the lad was aware of the term's base meaning, and was well-pleased with his contribution.

The silences impressed me; or rather, shook me, so I resolved that I would always speak of God to any young group I was instructing. In those days at Mass, we did not reply 'and with your spirit' to the priest's greeting of 'the Lord be with you'; we simply replied 'and with you'. Today at least, those attending any Mass have to confront the term regularly and perhaps pause and wonder what it means. In those far off days, hardly any students could speak usefully about God as spirit, or even about the spiritual. It was as though they were de facto materialists, although they knew God was not like Casper the friendly ghost.

So I always spoke of God as a powerful invisible force of love who created the entire universe and whose love for us was vitally important. The best place to start to understand God was their parents' love for them or their love for their parents. Nearly all of them knew what it was to be homesick, without the presence of their parents' love. Such love is powerful, necessary and good. I also explained the reality of powerful, invisible physical forces such as gravity and electricity.

These mixed examples give us some idea of the problems in speaking about God because human words do not fit God exactly. Sometimes the terms themselves are negative. Just as we start to explain spiritual by saying it is not material or physical, so infinite means cannot be measured and omnipotent means no limits to God's powers.

It was sometimes disconcerting, even occasionally hilarious as I asked them why I could not 'slam dunk' the basketball. Some youngsters would suggest I lacked the self-confidence to slam dunk (I explained I have plenty of self-confidence.) Others more correctly pointed out that I lacked the jumping ability and we eventually agreed that the force of gravity prevented me, although if we travelled to the moon, I would be able to slam dunk. Discussions about finding their way without a map and eventually nominating the compass and what force oriented the compass were more subdued, but still generally useful as background for a reasonable theism.

Human reason can take us some considerable distance towards God, but Jesus' teachings, especially his parables have given us many more useful insights into the reality and workings of the Transcendent, of the Mystery which lies behind the veil of physical reality.

We never know the fruits or consequences of what we write or speak, although the written word can remain for a long time and appear in distant places. The children I taught were nearly always well prepared, but I hope my few words produced at least a few additional seeds, which grew and endured.

The soil and the climate for Christian faith and morals in Australia are not conducive to rich harvests, but we must continue our attempts to plant. Probably many Australians don't know what they are missing, why they are uneasy, or what they are looking for. But tides always turn.

One unexpected development in Godliness, a blessing, is the enthusiasm of many young adults, especially at the university chaplaincies, for silent prayer before the Blessed Sacrament. The consecrated host is exposed on the altar, often in a beautifully decorated holder, called a monstrance, for silent meditation and adoration. This is usually preceded and concluded with the Rite of Benediction, a solemn blessing with the consecrated host, which is an ancient, medieval piety.

Such eucharistic devotions fell into disfavour in some quarters after the Second Vatican Council, so the contemporary enthusiasm of many youth was unexpected. It was as though in their noisy, distracted lives, young people felt the need for silence, and for adoration, for reverencing the Transcendent God. It could be that the spreading enthusiasm for the 'old Mass', the Tridentine rite, in Europe and the USA, not so much in Australia, also fills a need for regular worship, for quiet and contemplation, for acknowledging the vertical dimension in the liturgy.

Jesus Christ

Naturally enough for Catholics, prayer, worship, godly living according to the Ten Commandments are explicitly Christo-centric. Jesus Christ is not seen as simply the greatest of the prophets, an outstanding mystic, the most captivating teacher in all history.

Certainly, Jesus is seen to be our brother, the Son of Mary, the Jewish wife of Joseph, truly human, who lived among us, suffered with us, died for us. But he then rose again on the third day after his death because he is the only Son of God his Father; Joseph was not his natural father.

From the fact that Jesus is true God and true man, a number of important consequences follow. Being divine as well as human meant that Jesus could redeem all humanity through his suffering and death on the cross. His sacrifice is sufficient and reconciling so that every penitent sinner can be forgiven, including those who might have been among the worst moral monsters and believers and good people will be rewarded with heaven after death.

Catholics commemorate the redemption with regular acts of worship, celebrated in beautiful churches around the country on each Sunday in a ceremony which closely follows the ritual blessing of bread and wine, which Jesus celebrated on the night before he died. To the consternation of many of his followers, Jesus taught that the bread and wine become His Body and Blood, which his followers are to consume. This same great mystery of love is celebrated everywhere, in magnificent cathedrals with pomp and solemn music, in lively parish communities, and with tiny communities in small, isolated churches. This regular prayer is 'the source and summit' of Catholic life.

Because Jesus is truly divine, his teachings have a unique authority. As the Son of God, he has brought us the Maker's instructions. It is for this reason that all believers from the Pope down to a young child stand under the apostolic tradition as its servants and defenders. No one is its master.

This important belief helps us understand the tradition of the martyrs, their invincible loyalty, their determination not to compromise the supernatural treasures they have received, which open the Transcendent to all the faithful, to all of us.

Conclusion

The Catholic practices of worship and contemplation are rich and beautiful, embellished by the finest music, outstanding cathedrals, beautiful art and literature. But they are threatened from without and within. For the moment, in Australia the number of people without religion is increasing with the no-religion category exploding by 2,200,000 in the five years to 2016 to 30%. And our Australian situation is not untypical of much of the agnostic drift across the Western world.

In conclusion, I would like to resurrect a forgotten figure from forty years ago to have the last word: Aleksandr Solzhenitsyn whose writings about life in the Soviet prisons, the gulag, helped lay the foundations for the Communist collapse in Russia and Eastern Europe.

He believed that the disasters of twentieth century Russian history occurred because 'men have forgotten God'; indeed, he sees this as 'the principal trait of the entire 20th century.'

In 1983, he saw the threat to the faith in the Western world. He could have been writing about today. The symptoms of these dangerous threats are 'the abandonment of the concepts of good and evil and the rise of hatred'. 'Atheist teachers in the West are bringing up a younger generation in a spirit of hate for their own society.' This was decades before cancel culture and woke activists.

As a believer, Solzhenitsyn reassured us that 'the Creator constantly, day in and day out, participates in the life of each of us'.

This is true even in distant irreligious Australia, the lucky country. We too must realise that 'the Divine Spirit moves with no less force' among us also and we too should take Solzhenitsyn's advice and 'reach (out) with determination for the warm hand of God'.

George Pell was born in Ballarat, Victoria on 8 June 1941. Educated at Loreto Convent and St Patrick's College Ballarat. He entered Corpus Christi Seminary, Werribee in 1960 and was ordained in St Peter's Basilica in Rome in December 1966. He was educated at the Urban University in Rome at Oxford University and at Monash. He was Archbishop of Melbourne (1996–2001), Archbishop of Sydney (2001–2014) and Inaugural Prefect of the Secretariat for the Economy, Vatican City (2014–2019). He now divides his time between Sydney and Rome.

'UNDER GOD AND THE LAW' LIMITED GOVERNMENT AND CIVIL DISOBEDIENCE IN THE CHRISTIAN LEGAL TRADITION

AUGUSTO ZIMMERMANN

First Considerations

An important debate throughout Western legal history is whether a law, to be recognised as such, ought to conform to certain standards of justice and morality. Some legal theorists have answered this question in the affirmative, arguing for the existence of principles that are superior to the positive commands of the State. Whatever one might make of this, the fact is Western legal systems have been largely influenced by the moral convictions of Christian lawyers and politicians who believed in a higher or superior law that is above the law of the State. The belief in higher or superior laws has been enshrined in all the most celebrated documents in Western legal history, including the English *Magna Carta* (1215) and *Bill of Rights* (1689), the American *Declaration of Independence* (1776), and even the French *Declaration of the Rights of Man and the Citizen* (1789).

The idea of a higher law which protects the natural rights of the individual was first advocated by medieval scholars, then reshaped by the likes of John Locke and Thomas Jefferson, and then invoked in the 1960s in the struggle for civil rights in the United States, although it is true the judicial and political classes now completely ignore this important tradition of legality. In fact, those who appeal to this Christian legal tradition even risk being condemned. During his confirmation process in the Senate, Clarence Thomas of the U.S. Supreme Court was viciously attacked for merely explaining 'the higher law political philosophy of the Founding Fathers'.[1] As stated by Justice Thomas:

> ... natural rights and higher law arguments are the best defense of liberty and of limited government. Moreover, without recourse to higher law, we abandon our best defense of judicial review – a judiciary active in defending the Constitution, but judicious in its restraint and moderation. Rather than being a justification of the worst type of judicial activism, higher law is the only alternative to the wilfulness of both run-amok majorities and run-amok judges.[2]

St Augustine of Hippo is broadly recognised as one of the greatest Christian theologians to advocate for the higher law. He articulated a concept of the higher law that every government ought to act in strict conformity with. St Augustine believed in the existence of objective standards which make an unjust law 'not seen to be law at all'. When the State commands what is wrong, he concluded, the basic distinction between a government and a gang of criminals disappears. As the saint himself put it: 'Justice being taken away, then, what are kingdoms but great robberies? For what are robberies themselves, but little kingdoms?' The entire passage, which is found in *The City of God*, is rather illuminating

1 Clarence Thomas, 'Toward a Plain Reading of the Constitution – The Declaration of Independence in Constitutional Interpretation' (1987) 30 *Howard Law Journal* 691.
2 Clarence Thomas, 'The Higher Law Background of the Privileges or Immunities Clause of the Fourteenth Amendment' (1989) 12 *Harvard Journal of Law & Public Policy* 63, 64.

because it explains how a legitimate government can be distinguished from a criminal organisation:

> Justice being taken away, then, what are kingdoms but great robberies? For what are robberies themselves but little kingdoms? The band itself is made of men; it is ruled by the authority of a prince... the booty is divided by the law agreed on. If, by the admittance of abandoned men, this evil increases to such a degree that it holds places, fixes abodes, takes possession of cities and peoples, it assumes the more plainly the name of kingdom, because the reality is now manifestly conferred on it, not by the removal of covetousness, but by the addition of impunity. Indeed, that was an apt and true reply which was given to Alexander the Great by a pirate who had been seized. For when that king had asked the man what he meant by keeping hostile possession of the sea, he answered with bold pride, "What you mean by seizing the whole earth; but because I do it with a petty ship, I am called a robber, while you who do it with a great fleet are styled emperor".[3]

In the thirteenth century Franciscan monks were the first to elaborate sophisticated theories of God-given, inalienable rights of the individual. Those theologians connected these inalienable rights to a broader understanding of divine justice. The monks understood that the equal freedom of every individual is God's gift to all humanity. Original to those Franciscan thinkers was the belief in fundamental rights that are grounded in human dignity and must therefore be legally protected for the advancement of the common good. This theological perspective mandates human authority can never abrogate these inalienable rights of the individual, which are our basic rights to life, liberty and property.

In 1215, when King John of England was forced to sign the Magna

---

3 St Augustine of Hippo, *The City of God*, Bk IV, Pt 4.

Carta, the preamble explains the document was underpinned by a 'reverence for God and for the salvation of our souls and those of all our ancestors and heirs, for the honour of God and the exaltation of the Holy Church and the reform of our realm, on the advice of our reverent fathers'. A few years later, Henry de Bracton (d.1268), an influential royal judge, defined the meaning of jurisprudence as 'the science of the just and unjust', and the enforcement of laws 'a just sanction ordering virtue and prohibiting its opposite'.[4] This would lead Bracton to conclude that kings must invariably be under God and the law, because the law makes them kings. 'For there is no king where will rules rather than the law', he said. As noted by O.H. Phillips:

> Bracton, writing in the thirteenth century adopted the theory
> generally held in the Middle Ages that the world was governed by law,
> human or divine; and that "the King himself ought not be subject to
> man but subject to God and to the law, because the law makes him
> king". The same view is also expressed in the Year of Books of the
> fourteenth and fifteenth centuries. Such superior law governed kings
> as well as subjects and set limits to the prerogative. On that ground
> Fortescue, in the middle of the fifteenth century, based his argument
> that there could be no taxation without the consent of Parliament.[5]

Sir John Fortescue (1394–1476) was a chief justice of the King's See also:Bench during the reign of Henry VI. He was known to be a very good judge. In fact, Fortescue was highly recommended for his See also:wisdom and uprightness. In this context, tyranny was described by him as an attempt to undermine our natural desire for personal freedom, which Fortescue believed was instilled in the human heart by God himself. He goes on to quote from Mark 2:27 so as to explain how kings have been

4 Henry de Bracton, *On the Laws and Customs of England* (Cambridge/MA: Harvard University Press, 1968), 33
5 O.H. Phillips and P. Jackson, *Constitutional and Administrative Law* (7th Ed., London/UK: Sweet & Maxwell, 1993), 33

called by God to govern for the sake of the kingdom, not the other way around. Fortescue remarked:

> *A law is necessarily adjudged cruel if it increases servitude and diminishes freedom, for which human nature always craves. For servitude was introduced by men for vicious purposes. But freedom was instilled into human nature by God. Hence freedom taken away from men always desires to return, as is always the case when natural liberty is denied. So he who does not favour liberty is to be deemed impious and cruel.*[6]

Sir William Blackstone (1723-1780) was another important advocate of principles of constitutional government informed by inherent rights and freedoms. His *Commentaries on the Laws of England* (1765-69) were enormously influential, indeed the foundation for the entire American system of law and government. Blackstone's book also arrived with the First Fleet in 1788 and has had a significant impact on the evolution of the law in Australia. This book remains a seminal source regarding the classical views of the common law as a legal system. To avoid tyranny, Blackstone argues no law which contradicts God's natural laws must ever be considered valid. These natural laws, wrote Blackstone, acknowledge the existence of inalienable rights that are inherent in human nature as a gift of God to everyone, regardless of time and circumstances. That being so, Blackstone concluded:

> *No human laws should be suffered to contradict these natural laws... Nay, if any human law should allow or enjoin us to commit it, we are bound to transgress that human law, or else we must offend both the natural and the divine.*[7]

Above all, the notion that law must preserve freedom is an important legacy of Christianity. 'The law of the Lord is perfect, reviving the soul',

---

6 John Fortescue, *De Laudibus Legum Anglie* (Cambridge University Press, 1949) Chap. XLII, 105.
7 Sir William Blackstone, *The Sovereignty of the Law* (London/UK: McMillan, 1973), 58-9.

says the Psalmist (Psa 19:7). And God's law is also described in the Holy Bible as 'the perfect law of liberty' (Jas. 1:25). That being so, St Paul counsels his fellow Christians in Galatia to 'stand fast therefore in the liberty wherewith Christ hath made us free' (Gal. 5:1). St Paul also states 'There is neither Jew nor Greek, there is neither bond nor free, there is neither male nor female: for ye are all one in Christ Jesus' (Gal. 3.28). Statements like these had a profound impact on the development of democracy and human rights. Harold Berman credits these beliefs as having 'an ameliorating effect on the position of women and slaves and the protection of the poor and helpless' in Germanic law between the sixth and eleventh centuries.[8]

The leading opponents of slavery in eighteenth century England were Christians who had come to the view that since Adam and Eve were the first humans they were also the ancestors of black humans – 'are not Adam and Eve parents of us all?'. William Wilberforce (1759–1833) was only 25-years-old when he first served in Parliament, in 1780. Over many years Wilberforce repeatedly introduced an anti-slavery trade bill in the House of Commons, until his private bill was finally passed just two days before he passed away. Largely as a result of his tireless efforts the United Kingdom was the world's first modern nation to outlaw slavery. Sociology professor Alvin J. Schmidt explains:

> It is difficult to find a better example than Wilberforce to show the powerful effect the teachings and spirit of Christ have had in fighting the social sin of slavery. No proponent of abolition of slavery even accomplished more. Largely as a result of his indefatigable efforts, slavery came to a complete end in all of the British Empire's possessions by 1840, making it the first modern country to outlaw slavery.[9]

8 Harold Berman, *Law and Revolution: The Formation of the Western Legal Tradition* (Harvard University Press, 1983), 31.
9 Alvin Schmidt, *How Christianity Changed the World* (Zondervan, 2004), 278.

The Christian Doctrine of Separation of Powers

According to Scripture, governments are expected to accomplish only limited tasks. Their primary role is the protection of the innocent and punishment of the guilty (Romans 13:3-4). As long as a government does what is right, citizens should obey human authority. St Peter explains: 'Submit you for the Lord's sake to every authority instituted among men, whether to the king, as the supreme authority, or to governors, who are sent by him to punish those who do wrong and to commend those who do right' (1 Peter 2:13-14).

But history teaches power is able to corrupt a ruler's character and, as Lord Acton added, 'absolute power corrupts absolutely'. A government that disperses power is, therefore, better than one that gathers power into the hands of a few. Accordingly, the separation of powers into independent branches of government – executive , legislative, and judicial – works as a more effective protection against abuse of power. Each branch of government wields specific power and acts as a check and balance against the other branches so that the concentration of power, which is always inimical of freedom, can be prevented.

Charles-Louis de Secondat, Baron de La Brède et de Montesquieu, generally referred to as simply Montesquieu, was a French judge, historian, and political philosopher. He is the principal source of the doctrine of separation of powers which is implemented in many constitutions throughout the world. To restrain the abuse of power, he argued, 'it is necessary from the disposition of things that power should be a check to power'.[10] According to him, 'there is no liberty if the judiciary power be not separate from the legislative and executive'. And as Montesquieu also pointed out, 'when the legislative and executive powers are united in the same person, or in the same body of magistrates,

---

10 Charles Louis de Secondat, Baron de Montesquieu, *The Spirit of Laws* [1750] Bk XI, Ch.6.

there can be no liberty; because apprehensions may arise, lest the same monarch or senate should enact tyrannical laws, to execute them in a tyrannical manner'. As noted by David Barton:

> *This separation of powers theory [elaborated by Montesquieu] is rooted in the Biblical concept espoused in Jeremiah 17:9 that man naturally tends toward corruption. Following the religious teaching of the day, it was generally accepted that the unrestrained heart of man moved toward moral and civil degradation... Thus it was logical that society would be much safer if all power did not repose in the same authority. With the power divided, if one branch became wicked, the others might still remain righteous and thus be able to check the wayward influence.*[11]

Montesquieu's *L'Esprit Des Lois* (*The Spirit of the Laws*) was first published in 1747. Its first 1750 English translation became particularly popular in America. During the ratification debates for the U.S. Constitution, those who supported it and those who argued against it relied very heavily on Montesquieu's book to justify their positions. As noted by Jeremy Kirk, 'at the Constitutional Convention, no man was quoted more frequently than Montesquieu... It was from Montesquieu... that the Framers obtained a theory of checks and balances and of the division of powers'.[12]

The American Founders deliberately based their political system on Montesquieu's clear and rigid separation of the legislative, executive and the judicial branches of government; a concept which endures as fundamental to American constitutionalism. As such, Montesquieu's separation of powers' doctrine was considered vital to counteract the inherent problems related to our sinful ambitions for power and glory.

11 David Barton, *Original Intent* (Aledo/TX: Wallbuilders, 2005), 215.
12 Russell Kirk, *Rights and Duties: Reflections on our Conservative Revolution* (Dallas/TX: Spence Publishing Co., 1997),

Those writing the constitution believed in the inherently corruptibility of human nature and societies. As George Washington famously stated: 'A just estimate of that love of power and proneness to abuse it which predominates in the human heart, is sufficient to satisfy us for the truth of this position'. Thus Washington concluded: 'the importance of reciprocal checks in the exercise of political power by dividing and distributing it into different depositories... has been evinced'.[13]

The same premise concerning the necessity to separate the powers of the State was manifested by Alexander Hamilton in the *Federalist Paper No.15*: 'Why has government been instituted at all? Because the passions of men will not conform to the dictates of reason and justice without constraint... [T]he infamy of a bad action is to be divided among a number [rather] than... to fall singly upon one'.[14] Ultimately, the American Founders believed, because humans are inherently sinful, that it is dangerous to concentrate political power. They aimed at designing a model of constitutional framework that more rigidly would separate powers and create a variety of mechanisms whereby each branch of government would check the others.

The Christian Justification for Civil Disobedience

Christians are required by Scripture to first obey God and then human authorities. For example, when the Sanhedrin commanded Peter and John to stop talking about Christ, the apostles boldly responded: 'Judge for yourselves whether it is right in God's sight to obey man rather than God' (Acts 4:19). In fact, the Bible has many passages justifying the lawful right to resist political tyranny. They can be found in Exodus 1:17-21, Esther 3:2 and 4:13-16, Daniel 3:16-18, and Acts 5:29. This led the early Christian theologian, Origen (c 185–254), to conclude:

---

13 George Washington, Farewell Address (September 17, 1796), at https://www.loc.gov/resource/mgw2.024/?sp=242&st=text
14 Alexander Hamilton, *Federalist Paper No.15*

> *Where the law of nature, that is of God, enjoins precepts*
> *contradictory to the written laws, consider whether reason does not*
> *compel a man to dismiss the written code and the intention of the*
> *lawgivers, and to devote himself to the divine Lawgiver and to choose*
> *to live according to His word, even if in doing this he must endure*
> *dangers and countless troubles and death and shame.*[15]

To apparently defeat the Covid-19 virus that might be deadly only for those who are very old or seriously ill Australian politicians, especially Daniel Andrews in Victoria, have acquired extraordinary powers to impose draconian measures that have caused millions of people to endure highly stressful and traumatic situations, including home confinement, job losses, financial ruin, and a whole host of mental illnesses and challenges. These measures are unlawful according to the Christian tradition of government under the law as they have profoundly affected the enjoyment of our fundamental freedoms, including freedom of speech, association, movement, expression, and privacy.

The right to disobey unlawful measures that affect the enjoyment of our fundamental freedoms constitutes an old Christian tradition. In the seventeenth century, the celebrated Scottish theologian, Samuel Rutherford (1600-1661), stated in *Lex Rex* that a political power, whenever it is used to oppress, 'is not lawful but a licentious deviation of a lawful power'.[16] Of course, the American Founders had this in mind when they finally appealed to a 'long train of abuses' in order to justify their successful revolutionary actions. Drawing from John Locke's political writings, the *American Declaration of Independence* starts by manifesting that, 'whenever any form of government becomes destructive of these ends, it is the right of the people to alter or to abolish it, and to institute new government'. This particular statement is taken from Locke's *Second*

15 Origen, *Contra Celsum*, Bk 5, para 37
16 Samuel Rutherford, *'Lex Rex', or The Law and the Prince* – Vol. 3, 34, in: *The Presbyterian Armoury*, 1846.

Treatise on Civil Government, the following passage in particular:

> *Whenever the legislators endeavour to take away and destroy*
> *the property of the people [i.e., their basic rights to life, liberty, and*
> *property], or to reduce them to slavery under arbitrary power, they*
> *put themselves into a state or war with the people, who are thereupon*
> *absolved from any further obedience, and are left to the common refuge*
> *which God hath provided for all men against force and violence.*[17]

One of the Australia's leading legal academics, Gabriël Moens AM, explains that civil disobedience can potentially be justified whenever 'the normal channels of social change do not function properly anymore or whenever serious grievances are not heard'. As he points out, 'a system does not function adequately anymore when some groups have entrenched power positions in society and use their power to impose their will on weaker or vulnerable classes of people'. Although the right to disobey unjust law should preferably be non-violent, Professor Moens also reminds us that laws which violate our basic rights and freedoms are themselves 'more subtle forms of violence'.[18]

It goes without saying that any recourse to civil disobedience should be balanced against the principle of regular obedience to validly enacted laws. As a strong medicine to render the ruling classes more responsive to reasonable popular grievances, reliance on civil disobedience necessarily requires a long sequence of abuses and it should be followed by popular mobilisation coupled with widespread community support. Above all, a political system is said to no longer work properly whenever the normal channels of societal change have ceased to operate satisfactorily. Thus, leading to a situation where grievances are inflicted on the people by a ruling class that has become no more than an entrenched oligarchy. In this

---

17 John Locke, *Second Treatise of Government* (c 1681) ch 19, sec 222.
18 Gabriël A Moens AM, Enduring Ideas: Contributions to Australian Debates (Connor Court Publishing, 2020), 29.

case, civil disobedience becomes a perfectly valid and effective way to alter the oppressive status quo.

This view of our right to resist unjust law was particularly relevant during the civil rights movement in the United States during 1960s. Leading the fight against segregation was the legendary Baptist minister, Dr Martin Luther King Jr (1929-1968). When Dr King decided to peacefully march on Good Friday in 1963, a federal magistrate issued a writ on behalf of Birmingham City authorities prohibiting it. Dr King refused to comply with the writ and he was arrested as a result. Because he had asked citizens to respect judicial decisions that outlawed racial segregation, 'at first glance', he wrote in his solitary confinement and on stripes of a toilet paper: 'It may seem quite paradoxical for me consciously to break laws. One could ask how I could advocate breaking some laws and obeying others', to which Dr King replied:

> The answer lies in the fact that there are two types of laws: just and unjust. One has not only a legal but a moral responsibility to obey just laws. Conversely, one has a moral responsibility to disobey unjust laws. I would agree with St Augustine that an unjust law is no law at all. Now, what is the difference between the two? A just law is a man-made code that squares with the moral law or the law of God. An unjust law is out of harmony with the moral law. To put it in the terms of St Thomas Aquinas, an unjust law is a human law that is not rooted in eternal and natural law.[19]

In his celebrated fight against racial segregation Dr King established the Christian distinction between the formally legal and the objectively moral, which thereby allowed him to conclude that an unjust law may even be 'on the books', so to speak, but since it denies the fundamental rights to a segment of the population, this law must be disobeyed because it 'does

---

19 Martin Luther King Jr, *Why We Can't Wait* [1964] (New York/NY: Signet, 1996), pp 84–5.

not square with the law of God, so for reason it is unjust and any law that degrades the human personality is an unjust law'. Indeed, a significant part of Dr King's strategy to further the American civil rights movement was precisely to challenge unjust laws by measuring them in accordance with traditional Christian principles of legality. In this line of reasoning, to disobey an unjust law is to actually demonstrate an utmost respect and appreciation for the rule of law. Indeed, Dr King explained:

> *The individual who disobeys the law whose conscience tells him it is unjust, and who is willing to accept the penalty by staying in jail until that law is altered, is expressing at the moment the very highest respect for the law.*[20]

Final Considerations

The Christian teaching with the greatest implications for the protection of fundamental legal rights is the belief that because humanity is created in the image of God, all human beings are of equal worth in the sight of God. As Montesquieu noted in *The Spirit of the Laws*: 'The Christian religion, which ordains that we should love each other, would without doubt have every nation blest with the best civil, the best political laws; because these, next to this religion, are the greatest good that men can give and receive'.[21] Montesquieu also commented:

> *The mildness so frequently recommended in the Gospels, is incompatible with despotic rage with which a prince punishes his subjects, and exercises himself in cruelty. We owe to Christianity, in government a certain political law, and in war a certain law of nations, benefits which human nature can never sufficiently acknowledge.*[22]

20 James M Washington (ed.), *The Essential Writings and Speeches of Martin Luther King Jr.*, (New York/NY: HarperCollins, 1991), p 49
21 Montesquieu, *The Spirit of the Laws*, Bk XXIV, Ch. 3.
22 Ibid. Book XXIV, Chapter 3.

In this sense, the Christian tradition of limited government and lawful resistance to political tyranny must be regarded as essential for the preservation of our God-given, inalienable rights and freedoms. A tradition so important that Thomas Jefferson (1743-1826) asked rhetorically: 'Can the liberties of a nation be thought secure when we have removed their only firm basis, a conviction in the minds of the people that these liberties are the gift of God?'.[23] To answer this question, Jeffrie G. Murphie, an American legal philosopher, explains:

> *The rich moral doctrine of the sacredness, the preciousness, the dignity of persons cannot in fact be utterly detached from the theological context in which it arose and of which it for so long formed an essential part. Values come to us trailing their historical past; and when we attempt to cut all links to that past we risk cutting the life lines on which those values essentially depend. I think that this happens in... any attempt to retain all Christian moral values within a totally secular framework. Thus 'All men are created equal and are endowed by their Creator with certain inalienable rights' may be a sentence we must accept in an all or nothing fashion–not one where we can simply carve out what we like and junk the rest.[24]*

The late English economist and philosopher, William Aylott Orton (1889-1952), once commented it was not safe to assume the rights and freedoms we take for granted would persist if the religious faith and doctrine underpinning them and responsible for their birth were abandoned. In fact, it appears, in the long run, no effective protection to our inalienable rights can be sustained without the higher standards of justice and morality that were brought into the texture of Western

---

23 Thomas Jefferson, *Notes on the State of Virginia - Query XVIII: The particular customs and manners that may happen to be received in that state?* (1781), at http://xroads.virginia.edu/~hyper/jefferson/ch18.html

24 Jeffrie G. Murphy, 'Afterword: Constitutionalism, Moral Skepticism, and Religious Belief', *in* Alan S. Greenwood (ed.), *Constitutionalism: The Philosophical Dimension* (New York/NY: Greenwood Press, 1988), 249.

democracies by Christianity, not only as a school of thought but as a way of life and feeling: as a worldview, in short.[25] The testimony of history and the reality of current events prove Orton correct.

Augusto Zimmermann is Professor and Head of Law at the Sheridan Institute of Higher Education, and also Adjunct Professor of Law at the University of Notre Dame Australia (Sydney Campus). From 2012 to 2017, Augusto served as a Law Reform Commissioner in Western Australia. While teaching at Murdoch University, he was awarded the 2012 Vice Chancellor's Award for Excellence in Research. Augusto is also President of the Western Australian Legal Theory Association and Editor-in-Chief of the Western Australian Jurist law journal.

Short Bibliography

St AUGUSTINE of Hippo, The City of God (Penguin, 2004).

David BARTON, Original Intent (Aledo/TX: Wallbuilders, 2005).

Harold BERMAN, Law and Revolution: The Formation of the Western Legal Tradition (Harvard University Press, 1983).

Sir William Blackstone, The Sovereignty of the Law (London/UK: McMillan, 1973).

Henry de BRACTON, On the Laws and Customs of England (Cambridge/MA: Harvard University Press, 1968).

Edward S, CORWIN, The 'Higher Law' Background of American Constitutional Law (Cornell University Press, 1955).

John FORTESCUE, De Laudibus Legum Anglie (Cambridge University Press, 1949).

Mark David HALL, 'Vindiciae, Contra Tyrannos', in Daniel L. Dreisbach and Mark David Hall (eds.), Faith and the Founders of the American Republic (Oxford University Press, 2014)

Alexander HAMILTON, James Madison and John Jay, The Federalist Papers (New York/NY: Mentor Books, 1961).

---

25 William Aylott Orton, *The Liberal Tradition*: A Study of the Social and Spiritual Conditions of Freedom (new Haven/CT: Yale University Press, 1945), 57

Thomas JEFFERSON, Notes on the State of Virginia - Query XVIII: The particular customs and manners that may happen to be received in that state? (1781), at http://xroads.virginia.edu/~hyper/jefferson/ch18.html

Martin Luther KING Jr, Why We Can't Wait [1964] (New York/NY: Signet, 1996)

John LOCKE, Political Writings (Penguin Books, 1993).

Gabriël MOENS, Enduring Ideas: Contributions to Australian Debates (Connor Court Publishing, 2020).

Charles Louis de Secondat, Baron de Montesquieu, The Spirit of Laws [1750]

Jeffrie G. MURPHY, 'Afterword: Constitutionalism, Moral Skepticism, and Religious Belief', in Alan S. Greenwood (ed.), Constitutionalism: The Philosophical Dimension (New York/NY: Greenwood Press, 1988), p 249.

O.H. PHILLIPS and P. Jackson, Constitutional and Administrative Law (7th Ed., London/UK: Sweet & Maxwell, 1993).

Martin Luther King Jr, Why We Can't Wait [1964] (New York/NY: Signet, 1996), pp 84–5.

Russell KIRK, Rights and Duties: Reflections on our Conservative Revolution (Dallas/TX: Spence Publishing, Co, 1997).

William Aylott ORTON The Liberal Tradition: A Study of the Social and Spiritual Conditions of Freedom (new Haven/CT: Yale University Press, 1945).

Alvin SCHMIDT, How Christianity Changed the World (Zondervan, 2004), 278.

Clarence THOMAS, 'Toward a Plain Reading of the Constitution — The Declaration of Independence in Constitutional Interpretation' (1987) 30 Howard Law Journal 691.

Clarence THOMAS, 'The Higher Law Backgroound of the Privileges or Immunities Clause of the Fourteenth Amendment' (1989) 12 Harvard Journal of Law & Public Policy 63, 64.

George WASHINGTON, Farewell Address (September 17, 1796), at https://www.loc.gov/resource/mgw2.024/?sp=242&st=text

James Melvin WASHINGTON (ed.), The Essential Writings and Speeches of Martin Luther King Jr. (New York/NY: HarperCollins, 1991).

LITERATURE, MUSIC AND THE ARTS

PETER CRAVEN

It would be a sad thing if our culture lost its sense of the Judeo-Christian tradition which has shaped it and by whose light it has often had an abiding sense of direction, a faith to affirm, a symbology to draw strength from, a deep sense of the mystery. In the late '60s, Tom Kenneally published a novel *Three Cheers for the Paraclete* in which the liberal priest hero was said to be based on Ed Campion, the Riverview and Cambridge-educated man of God who always seemed to walk the ways of the world. He started his career on the staff of Cardinal Gilroy at St Mary's Cathedral and he went on to become Professor of Church History at St. Patrick's College, Manly where among a myriad of other aspirants to clerical rectitude he taught Tony Abbott and said it was like having a whale in a wading pool.

Ed Campion is in the habit of telling stories against himself and one of these is how when he saw Mother Teresa in Australia in the 1980s he said to her, 'I worked for you in Calcutta in the 1950s', and she, unblinking and unimpressed, with no affability or bonhomie said, 'When are you coming back?'. Ed remarked that saints were like that, they had no small talk. Edmund Campion, by contrast, has always talked the talk. How many clerics would have been sufficiently uncloistered to have written this description of the younger days of that uncompromising art critic and supreme celebrator in *The Fatal Shore* of our convict inheritance,

Robert Hughes? 'Robert Hughes used adjectives the way the chefs of Normandy use butter'. A sentence that resembles Hughes in its command of metaphor which avoids adjectival excess altogether.

Do we believe in a religion because of its cathedrals, its synagogues, its mosques, its temples?

Well, why not? If we endow art with that depth of moral being, that truth there is no arguing with, then why wouldn't we? The soaring abstract structure of a great cathedral is as much an expression of the injunction to love the Lord thy God with thy whole heart and thy whole soul and thy whole mind as are the polyphonic complexities and colorations of a mass by Palestrina, another of Campion's enthusiasms and touchstones.

It was John Henry Newman, the man who suborned the very word Oxford to connote a tilt back to the Catholic bedrock in nineteenth century Christianity when he launched the Oxford movement, who wrote of the beauty of holiness. And it was Newman who James Joyce (who would write the most comprehensive English language epic of the high modernist movement during that period a century or so ago – 1922 was the annus mirabilis we look back on as our renaissance moment when he wrote *Ulysses*) thought was the greatest of English prose stylists. In the 'Oxen of the Sun' chapter of his Bloomsday book, the chapter when they're waiting for a baby to be born, he crumples up all the styles of the past like so much tissue paper but some sparkle of eloquence escapes in his homage to Newman. 'Sins, or let us call them as the world calls them, unhappy memories.'

Ulysses is the epic by terms comic and tawdry and many-storied of Leopold Bloom, the unconscious Odysseus figure, who asserts the value of 'Love. I mean, the opposite of hatred' who defies the chauvinistic Citizen and says, 'Your Savior was a Jew like me'. It would be wrong to try to claim Joyce for the religion he tried to cast off. There's the whole retrospective mini-drama of Stephen Dedalus refusing to kneel down and pray at his mother's deathbed but there's that young man's questing tenuous voice in which he talks about 'amor matris: subjective and objective genitive' – the deep paradox of the love of a mother and the question 'What is the word known to all men?' which seems according to the greatest of Joyce's textual scholars, Hans Walter Gabler, to be simply, 'love'.

And all the vast and variegated voices of a Catholic Christianity shadow and enshroud the book at every point. Think of the quotation from Augustine that might seem to encapsulate the vision of *Ulysses* if it were susceptible to labels which could be stuck upon it. 'It was revealed to me that those things are good which yet are corrupted which neither if they were supremely good nor unless they were good could be corrupted.'

It has an extraordinary pertinence, no less pertinent for being limited, to the way we gauge the power of the sense of limitation in this book which does one thing, then another, in a series of virtuosic rehearsals of linguistic impoverishment which is also a testament to the riches of the earth, the Muse-like power that can roll and lilt from the mouth of the half-awake, half-drowsing Molly Bloom.

Before her, though, a spectral trinitaranism seems to brood over the fused vision of Bloom and Stephen as they behold 'the heaventree of stars hung with humid night-blue fruit'. And the whole coming together of the hopeless young James Joyce figure 'with a great future behind him' and his meeting with Leopold Bloom, the 'cultured, allround man' – who has no general culture, no education to speak of, but a depth of charity that speaks from the heart of the tradition we cherish – plays very deliberately on all that his/not his stuff in such a way as to suggest that the Holy Spirit is the divinity Joyce seeks to emulate though he can only do this as a fantastically learned and elaborate joke.

Buck Mulligan, his medico mate, had his point when he said that Stephen, Joyce's alter-ego, had the cursed Jesuit strain in him only it was injected the wrong way, almost as if the profundity of Joyce's

Catholicism which so impressed T.S. Eliot (who thought *Ulysses* ranked with Proust) – was as present like everything else in the book – by a principle of parody as if it were a designer drug, rather than the simplifying grace of a simple faith.

But think of that poem, the single one that escapes, even as it exemplifies, the 'slight lyric grace' of Joyce's poems.

> **Ecce Puer**
> *Of the dark past*
> *A child is born;*
> *With joy and grief*
> *My heart is torn…*
>
> *A child is sleeping:*
> *An old man gone.*
> *O, father forsaken,*
> *Forgive your son!*

It was written to commemorate the birth of Joyce's son and the death of his father. Imagine calling a poem 'Ecce Puer' ('Behold the boy') when the echo is of Pilate's desperate cry 'Ecce homo' ('Behold the man') the cry to the crowd asking them to pity Jesus only to get in return the cry of 'Crucify him! Crucify him!'

The poem has a supreme modesty, an absolute economy, unashamed of any lameness. It tallies with the Joyce who could admire the late stark Tolstoy story 'How Much Land Does A Man Need?'. (Answer: enough to be buried in.)

And a reference to Tolstoy is a reminder of how the author of *Anna Karenina* and *War and Peace*, of *Master and Man* and *The Death of Ivan Ilyich* in some sense transcends the consummate and comprehensive portrait he gives of an infinitely variegated nineteenth century world. If we compare Tolstoy, whether at his most epical or in the later stories and novellas, with his great French and English contemporaries, with Balzac and Flaubert, with Dickens and George Eliot, we are conscious – sometimes subliminally and sometimes with an insistent vehemence – that he is a religious writer and a Christian one. It's not simply that epigraph to *Anna Karenina* ("'vengeance is mine" saith the Lord, "I will repay'") but the overwhelming impulse to sum up the world according to a moral and metaphysical reckoning.

This is not what can make Tolstoy seem like the greatest of novelists but it is inseparable from his greatness. It's true that a writer who could virtually discover at least the effect of stream-of-consciousness technique (while never technically swerving from an overt omniscient form as Anna glides distracted to her death) would have been incomparably great whatever he believed or disavowed, but Tolstoy had God in his sights and everything about him is shaped by this. He quarrels with the Orthodox Church, he behaves appallingly to his wife, he rushes blindly he knows not where like a latter day King Lear, but he's bent on truth and his work demonstrates this at a level of triumph.

George Steiner, that polymath literary enthusiast, wrote a book about Tolstoy and his great contemporary Dostoyevsky suggesting Tolstoy was like that inventor of epic, Homer, whereas Dostoyevsky was the heir to Shakespeare's dramatic vision. Memories can underline this. The brogueless Anglo-Irish voice of the Jesuit retreat master, still clad in that Sorbonne gown worn as a gesture against British persecution, saying, 'My dear boys', the French philosopher Jean-Paul Sartre says, 'Hell is other people'. This in my opinion is completely wrong. On the contrary, I think Dostoyevsky was right when he said, 'Hell is the suffering of not being able to love'.

The vision in Dostoyevsky is tragic and he turns the novel into his stage, his intrinsically dramatic medium, but there's no mistaking the origins or the coloration of the mythology and metaphysic behind this.

Michel Foucault, indeed, says we do not glimpse the image of the suffering face of Christ from the seventeenth century – the moment of the later and greatest Shakespeare – and the latter part of the nineteenth century when Raskolnikov says to Sonya, 'I killed myself, not the old woman'.

Is it a paradox that the supreme master of drama and of suspense, of the thriller transfigured into the highest art, should be this epileptic compulsive gambler whose Slavophile political vision was more than a little crazed but whose dramatic grasp of *lacrimae rerum*, of the tears in things, to borrow the old phrase of Virgil who Dante would choose to lead him through the afterlife, is grounded in a sense of the constant need for contrition and the abiding faith in mercy. It is amusing that Dostoyevsky should have said in his journals, 'I'm not very good at singing lullabies but I've tried that too' because we do not automatically think of being soothed to sleep by megalomaniac and unhinged axe murderers, by the terrorists of *The Possessed* – who, as Edmund Wilson admitted, captured the horrific side of the Bolsheviks – in the novel the Russian formalist Bakhtin sees as polyphonic and whose polyphony hypothetically includes a hellish chapter about the cold blooded rape of a child. Or by the supreme frailty of Myshkin, the Prince in *The Idiot*, or by the man of storm and darkness, Rogozin who is his contrast and counterpoint. Think of *The Brothers Karamazov* where in the fable of the Grand Inquisitor we hear again the supreme wickedness of the false priest who can say, 'It is expedient that one man die for the sake of the nation'. And then the berserk supremely killable father and his sons – the man of headlong action Dmitri, his brother Ivan, who can comprehend the finer point of anything but is still confronted with spectral images of iniquity and then there is the saintly young brother Alyosha and that very creepy character Smerdyakov.

And through the whole towering, sometimes inaccessible gauntness and grandeur of *The Brothers Karamazov* there is the image not just of the atrocious face of paternity and the sometimes-deranged face of love, but the colossal capacity for human suffering. Remember how Father Zossima, the old saint, bows down on the ground when he acknowledges this capacity in Dimitri. Hitchcock said to Truffaut that he could never film *Crime and Punishment* because Dostoyevsky's vision meant too much to him. It is one of the ironies of recent literary culture – it was certainly true in the '60s and '70s – that a generation of adolescents who rejected the pieties of their parents and the morality and belief system that went with it – should have found themselves enthralled by Dostoyevsky with his exalted sense of election as crucifixion. Wasn't it Christopher Isherwood's swami who had never read a novel in his life and stumbled on *The Brothers Karamazov*, who said to the Englishman in search of spirituality in California, 'Ah! Are all novels about truth and mindfulness like this?'. Or words to that effect.

It's clear from George Pell's prison journals that he's an active believer in the crucifixionary aspect of Catholicism in its conservative mode, in a way that is older and more deeply grounded than his own experience but not incompatible with it. He does mention the Oxford classicist and sometime Jesuit the late Peter Levi who argued him into the ground on Vietnam one day in Campion Hall, and who preached with a Donne like grandeur at the funeral of that great Catholic convert poet David Jones whose First World War long prose poem *In Parenthesis* T.S. Eliot published and whose *The Anathemata* Auden thought was the greatest long poem of the twentieth century. Levi said that David Jones thought there were a lot of people who were in the Church without realising they were in it.

This is a perspective a little like that of Anthony Fisher, the Catholic Archbishop of Sydney, who said there was a *Finnegans Wake*, Here Comes Everybody aspect to the complex variegations, the catholicity of the infinitely divers folk who believed in the power, maybe even the glory, of what the Catholic caper could offer. It's no kind of argument but it's worth noting nonetheless that when Cardinal Pell was charged with historic sexual offences the liberal Catholics who had always been passionately resistant to his variety of muscular Christianity with its confidently vaunted moralisms and anathemas, immediately saw that the charges were trumped up and should never have been brought. They were staunch in their support of Pell, appalled by the failure of his appeal to the Victorian Court of Appeal and passionately approving of Justice Weinberg's dissenting judgement and the High Court's ultimate dismissal of the charge.

The Jesuit lawyer and Rector of Newman College Frank Brennan and the writer Gerard Windsor are public examples of this. But in practice it was a one to one map. The liberal Micks – however at home with every secularist and liberal approximation to the question of religion (and with it a latitudinarian attitude to sexuality, for instance) – knew far too much about the Catholicism that had formed them to believe a word of this always shady set of charges pursued so relentlessly by a police force which had itself connived in the covering up of child sexual abuse.

We need, of course, due caution when we are making the case for Christian, let alone Catholic, perspectives when it comes to art in general and literature in particular.

It's true that there is a strong case for seeing Gerard Manley Hopkins, Catholic convert and Jesuit, as the greatest poet of the Victorian period (not least because he is such a proto-modernist). This was the position of Leavis, of Empson, and it was the position of, say, Simon During (late of Melbourne, Johns Hopkins', wherever.) Hopkins' lyric poems like 'The Windhover' or 'Hurrahing the Harvest' are the greatest thing of their kind since Keats and they are different from Keats because there's a richness of tension in them because their vision is sacramental and Catholic. Hopkins' sprung rhythm and what Donald Davie called his unrestricted proto-Shakespearean diction (where, as it were, any word in the language can crop up) make him utterly remarkable technically and there is also meaning in every note of his music.

> *I caught this morning morning's minion, kingdom of daylight's*
> *dauphin, dapple-dawn-drawn Falcon, in his riding*
> *Of the rolling level underneath him steady air...*

Fifty years ago claims were made for Hopkins' 'Spring and Fall' as the most perfect, the least imperfect poem in the language:

> *Márgarét, áre you gríeving*
> *Over Goldengrove unleaving?*
> *Leáves like the things of man, you*
> *With your fresh thoughts care for, can you?*
> *Ah! ás the heart grows older*
> *It will come to such sights colder*
> *By and by, nor spare a sigh*
> *Though worlds of wanwood leafmeal lie;*
> *And yet you wíll weep and know why.*
> *Now no matter, child, the name:*
> *Sórrow's spríngs áre the same.*
> *Nor mouth had, no nor mind, expressed*
> *What heart heard of, ghost guessed:*
> *It ís the blight man was born for,*
> *It is Margaret you mourn for.*

And then there are the tragic sonnets: 'O the mind, mind has mountains; cliffs of fall / Frightful, sheer, no-man-fathomed. Hold them cheap / May who ne'er hung there.'

Those extraordinary intensities and extensions of 'I wretch lay wrestling with (My God!) my God' are poems of dire psychological calamity and premonition, brilliantly dynamized and with an intense dramatic coloration that is breathtaking. They are the Psalms and darker Shakespearean sonnets for an age to come which will mask melancholy under the new name of depression as one of its defining qualities. And the poems that are, by association, part of the dark or light of this aspect of Hopkins, have extraordinary tonal range – ' Thou art indeed just, Lord' – which paraphrases Jeremiah is a poem that takes it up to God, has its reckoning with the Most High as surely as Shakespeare does with his Golden Boy, his Youth, in Sonnet 94: 'They that have power to hurt and will do none.'

It is as if Hopkins prefigured by power of prophecy the age that could applaud him and he also gives us the triumph and spiritual revelation of 'That Nature is a Heraclitean Fire' as well as that beautifully assured traditional poem in which he does otherwise.

> *...O then if in my lagging lines you miss*
> *The roll, the rise, the carol, the creation,*
> *My winter world, that scarcely breathes that bliss*
> *Now, yields you, with some sighs, our explanation.*

But Hopkins whose Catholicism is integral to his greatness as a poet knew he had peers who did otherwise. He said once that he was sure Walt Whitman was a great scoundrel and there was no man he more resembled. And the analogous figure in French poetry is Rimbaud. The street boy who begins with a supreme mastery of the alexandrine and who will write 'I is an other' ('Je est un autre') – who leads his reader through the circus of his sordidness – 'as if I alone have the key to the barbarous sideshow' ('parade sauvage') – is the great French modernist avant la letter – in the latter part of the nineteenth century, parallel to Hopkins, though he drove poor Verlaine to try to shoot him and ended up long after he had forsworn poetry as a gunrunner.

Poetry doesn't have metaphysical favourites. Les Murray in Australia deserves his reputation as the greatest poet the brown land has seen in the longest time, and as an impassioned Catholic convert he dedicated all his poems 'ad majorem dei gloriam' ('to the greater glory of God') yet his contemporary Peter Porter – expatriated, discountenanced by the depth of the culture he embraced and with no religious faith, can seem the greater poet when he writes out of the heart of the blackness all around him. The terrible poems about the suicide of his wife which proffer no consolation are far beyond Murray's emotional range. 'The fire will come out of the sun / and I shall look into the heart of it.' Poetry of this power commands faith and cannot be subordinated to any particular variety.

And so it is with the great novels of the last hundred years. Yes, *Ulysses* recapitulates the vision of a Catholicism that becomes central to the book's human comedy but in Proust's *À la recherche du temps perdu* the active quest for time lost, the cult of memory and the recreating resurrectionary power of art become rival mythologies of extraordinary authority. The moral grandeur of what is created is in no way inferior to Joyce's: in fact Proust in his vast triumphant length with his soaring attitude and tone as well as the reduction of a vast solid world (and the encompassing of the Dreyfus case et cetera) is probably the greater work of literature.

Clearly there are different ways of looking at these things – through the prism of religious faith and not. One of the greatest modernist novels, Robert Musil's *The Man Without Qualities* has little truck with Christianity though the latter movement of this huge unfinished novel is headed in the direction of mysticism. Again with Thomas Mann we seem far from any Christian intimation at first though with the later Mann, the immense tetralogy *Joseph and His Brothers* is the supreme attempt to give a biblical story, the very beautiful Joseph story, a local habitation and a name – as well as a dazzling modern erudition – and linguistically the recourse to Luther's German broods over the book's diction as it does in *Doctor Faustus,* which is Mann's account of the diabolic pact, a parable of the Nazi nightmare in the context of icon-shattering musical innovation.

But all of this is difficult to get a general perspective on. If we live in a post-Christian period it's interesting how residually Christian it remains.

T.S. Eliot, the most influential critic as well as one of the greatest poets of the period, was an adherent to Anglo Catholic theology. Still, where *Ash Wednesday* is full of the cadences of liturgy, used to plangent effect, *Four Quartets* was published shorn of the scholarly arcana that functioned partly to disguise the profound dissociation of the state depicted in *The Waste Land*. But *Four Quartets,* which is a great poet's attempt to depict the experience of religious faith, is agnostically expressed. And it's instructive that in the case of Yeats' poetry – which has claims to surpass Eliot's just as it was Joyce's fear that the older Irishman might be the greater writer – the mystical syncretism that informed his work – exploring, as he suggested, a possible wisdom and a possible ecstasy – come across as more mainstream than their sources might suggest.

And there is plenty for the Catholic who wants homeside signposts to be getting on with. Ford Maddox Ford's *Parade's End* is by a Catholic of sorts and the later Evelyn Waugh, the Waugh of *Brideshead Revisited* and *The Sword of Honour* sequence, are explicitly Catholic. Two of the greater masters of literary form as supreme economy, Muriel Spark, the Scotswoman, and Flannery O'Connor, an American Southerner, were deep-dyed Catholics. And the Melbourne University philosophy professor Tony Coady was just one of innumerable co-religionists who believed that some form of anti-Catholicism must have led to Graham Greene failing to get the Nobel Prize for Literature for that extraordinary spate of novels from *The Power and the Glory* to *A Burnt Out Case* through the comic novels like *Our Man in Havana, Travels with my Aunt* and *Monsignor Quixote.*

Something in Greene pays homage to the sort of desolation and disquietude of a Jansenist sense of moral scruple but he dramatizes this with great power and it's fascinating that Greene could do this while having the momentum and readability of a thriller writer. He was one of nature's storytellers yet he reverted to that oldest story, the story of the Fall.

It's also true that Catholicism can be a dogmatic narrowness. It was that brilliant latter-day convert James McAuley – a fine traditional poet when he shed the modernism that had once been in him by parodying it in the Ern Malley poems – who tried to steer Patrick White (much the greatest writer Australia has produced) in the direction of Rome and our Nobel Prize winner replied that he must climb the mountain alone and we applaud this. Yet an old priestly headmaster was heard to remark of Patrick White – who, God knows, was a seeker all his days, 'But if he can do it by himself, where does that leave blokes like me?'

Where indeed? Somewhere in the dark wood, in the middle of the way, the direct way, lost to smithereens.

2021 was the year of Dante, the 700th anniversary of the death of the man who took the majesty of the medieval vision of Christianity and gave it a Renaissance vibrancy and such undreamt of individual faces and voices. Francesca saying of Paolo, 'La bocca mi baciò tutto tremante' (He kissed my mouth all trembling). The terrible signpost on Hell's gate, 'Lasciate ogni speranza, voi ch'entrate' (Abandon hope all ye who enter here.). The humorous soul in the Purgatorio who calls out to his betters, 'On you valiant'– no mountain climbing for him. And then the vision of the madonna, 'Vergine madre, figlia del tuo figlio' (Virgin Mother, daughter of your son). The merest vowel shift in the Tuscan Italian indicating universes of metamorphosis. And then the ultimate vision of 'L'amor che move il sole e l'altre stelle' ('The love that moves the sun and the other stars').

Dante is as great or greater than any poet who ever lived and his great *Commedia* seems to be cognate with a vision of Catholicism older than time itself.

It's easy, too easy, to see Dante's religious vision as just cultural wrapping paper. That when we gaze at the extraordinary authority of the beauty in a Raphael madonna or the enigmatic wisdom of a Leonardo, the vision only happens to be Christian. It doesn't, it's intrinsic. When we stare at the Sistine Chapel ceiling or listen to Mozart's *Requiem* or his *Coronation Mass* we are not experiencing the rhetoric of a religious vision but an essence where beauty and truth are at one. Think of the sublimity of Piero della Francesca's resurrected Christ, think of the majesty and the dolour and of the thing which rises beyond the sorrow of the world in Bach's *Saint Matthew Passion*.

Of course any person with a feeling for sound or image, for music or painting or literature will at least admit they are suspending their disbelief, but is that really what they're doing? Think of that poignant New Testament line, 'Lord, I believe: help thou my unbelief'. Remember that line in Shakespeare's *The Winter's Tale* when the statue of Leontes' dead wife Hermione comes to life and Paulina, the old wisewoman – marvellously incarnated by the great actress Dame Peggy Ashcroft, you can listen to her on the Caedmon recording – says, 'It is required you do awake your faith'. And isn't it at least feasible that this is how great religious art works its magic upon us? My dear friend Bill Henson, who brings to his photographs the compositional quality of great painting, says that he thinks the only kind of thinking worth doing is 'magical thinking'.

After all, the greatest art, the greatest literature and music, partakes of the nature of miracle. In marble, in print, using a bit of paint, with a few notes. How do they do it? John Jones, the Oxford Hegelian said of the confession moment in *Crime and Punishment*, 'God knows how the dull words do it but they do'. It's all in the domain of Tertullian's *Credo quia impossibile* and then its refinement in St. Anselm's ontological *Credo quia absurdum* (I believe because it is absurd).

None of which is to deny the barbarism, as Walter Benjamin always said, that accompanies every step of our civilisation. Athens executed Socrates, Rome executed Christ (both against their better judgements, which makes it worse). Part of the extraordinary moral dignity of the

Hebrew Bible is the depth of its self-reproach and the dramatisation of everything that is base. When Helen Garner read through the Bible in its entirety she said, 'There is great wisdom and great meanness'. The meanness is there over and over, it's made juridical in Deuteronomy and its cousins. Think of the extraordinary horror in that beautiful 'Rivers of Babylon' Psalm, 137.

One of the greatest lines in the history of the literature of the world, sacred and profane, is that line of impassioned loyalty, 'Jerusalem if I forget thee may my right hand lose her cunning'.

And remember that terrible vaunt at the end? 'Happy he shall be, who taketh and dashes thy little ones upon the stones'.

Over and over in the historical books, sometimes involving heroical good guys like Joshua, there are unflinching and self-satisfied stories about killing men, women, children. Ezra Pound, great poet and deluded political partisan, said of the Old Testament that it was full of 'black evil', to which Harold Bloom replied 'Black evil! You call that a Western mind'. But there is black evil, and we need simply to accept that in the most comprehensive book – excelling in range the whole of Shakespeare – the book that contains the erotic lyricism of the Song of Songs, the desolation of Job, the scarifying scepticism of the wisdom of Ecclesiastes and the overpowering grief of David as he weeps for his son, 'O my son Absalom, my son, my son Absalom! would God I had died for thee, O Absalom, my son, my son!' – every kind of grace and ghastliness will be encompassed.

You can listen to a complete recording of the Hebrew Bible in the King James Version and harken to its horrors, to its lamentations, to its griefs. Listening to Isaiah and the story of the man despised and rejected it's hard not to see it as a prefiguration of Christ (and not simply because Handel's *Messiah* encourages us to).

The New Testament is part of the air we breathe and may it ever be. 'Blessed are the poor in spirit, for theirs is the kingdom of heaven'... 'Can anything good come out of Nazareth?'... 'What is truth?'... 'Thou art Peter, and upon this rock I will build my church'... 'Father, forgive them, for they know not what they do'... 'I am the resurrection and the life.'

Does it matter that Caravaggio peoples his great paintings of religious drama with street boys and working girls, that the Church over and over again asked for the vengeance of heaven? Not essentially.

Shakespeare, when he was writing his plays, lived in a time of axe-edge religious controversy and hideous threat. Thomas More who wrote *Utopia* had been executed, Cranmer, who wrote the *Book of Common Prayer* had been burnt alive. Shakespeare – the great Harvard scholar Harry Levin thought Elizabethan England was Catholic in its deepest sensibilities – sidestepped all this, all this religious dissension and deliberation. But in the last moments of *The Tempest*, when Prospero, the magician, asks for our applause, it's the Lord's Prayer he invokes – isn't it? – the 'debita nostra, sicut et nos dimittimus debitoribus nostris', the 'forgive us our trespasses' of the Pater noster, the Our Father.

> *As you from crimes would pardon'd be*
> *Let your indulgence set me free.*

Peter Craven is one of Australia's best-known literary critics. He edited Scripsi with Michael Heyward and was the founding editor of the Black Inc. Best Of annuals (Essays, Stories, Poems) and of Quarterly Essay. His work appears regularly in the Age, Australian, Sydney Morning Herald *and* Australian Literary Review. *He is a regular contributor of the Australian edition of the* Spectator. *He has also written extensively about theatre, film and television.*

Universities

Stephen Chavura

The purpose of the university

The university is the only European institution that has maintained its essential pattern and social function throughout modern history. Furthermore, no other European institution has spread over the world in its traditional form in the way the university has done.

Our word 'university' comes from the Latin *universitas*, meaning 'the whole' or 'the totality'. It was, in fact, a word commonly used by medieval jurists to denote any kind of organisation. But more specifically, the universities were described as a particular kind of *universitas*: a *universitas magistrorum et scholarium*—a university of teachers and students in pursuit of wide-ranging teaching and learning or *studium generale*.

Furthermore, a university is a space where one should be able to encounter the totality of known and knowable truth. In other words, at the very foundation of the university is a belief in truth with a capital T. Objective truth. Truth is not a social construct, it is true for anyone, regardless of whether any particular individual believes it or not. And if the apprehension of truth is the goal of a university, it should not surprise us once universities become full of scholars who either deny the existence of objective truth or subordinate its pursuit to other ends, such as economic prosperity, justice or power, universities or at least certain departments will decay. In this respect every university would do well to have engraved over its entryway the words of T. S. Eliot, that a university education is committed to 'the preservation of learning, for the pursuit of truth, and is so far as men are capable of it, the attainment of wisdom'.

This brief essay will first look at the Christian origins of the modern university, and how the university itself arose as an institutional expression of the Christian tradition of faith working with reason. Then the essay will turn to the problems in the modern university, and finally point to a way forward. Anyone who finds this contribution interesting should read Sir Roger Scruton's definitive essay 'The End of University' from *First Things* (April 2015).

Christianity and the university

Historian Edward Grant in his *Foundations of Modern Science in the Middle Ages* argues that an appreciation of wide learning and, in particular science, accompanied early Christian traditions. This was because Christianity itself arose in a Hellenised culture which was itself deeply invested in learning. Hellenistic philosophy sought to come to terms with the nature of reason or *logos*, and then to learn how to live according to it. Thus, John begins his gospel with language designed to prick the ears of the inquisitive in the Hellenised world: 'In the beginning was the Logos [Word], and the Logos was with God, and the Logos was God' (John 1:1). Cryptic to today's readers, less so to the literate in the Hellenistic world.

The Apostle Paul modelled the relationship between Christianity and secular learning. While speaking of the risen Jesus to Athenians he was called a babbler. Thus, when he was taken to the Areopagus, where philosophers would gather to exchange ideas, he acknowledged the religiosity of the Athenians and began his sermon by drawing his audience's attention to a shrine 'to an unknown God', and then proceeded to tell them who this God unknown to the Greeks was, quoting the Greek poet Epimenides in the oration (Acts 17:18-28). In other words, Paul himself was conversant with wider Greek learning and was happy to use it to communicate Christian truth to his pagan audience.

The greatest theologian of the ancient church, St Augustine, ornamented his dozens of books with references to ancient philosophers and scholars. Few in the ancient world were as conversant with Roman literature as St Augustine. It is true that some early Christians, like Tertullian, asked what Christianity could have to do with secular learning. But Augustine argued a capacity to discover the truth was a common gift God endowed on all people, and that much truth was to be found in non-Christian learning. According to Augustine in his *On Christian Doctrine*, 'if those who are called philosophers, especially the Platonists, have said what is true and in harmony with our faith, we are not only not to shrink from it, but to claim it for our own use…'. Following the example set by the Apostle Paul, for Augustine all truth is God's truth, and wide learning was eminently worthy of study for the light it sheds on Christian truth.

With the fall of the Roman Empire in AD476 one of the great projects was to protect and preserve Christian learning, particularly given the threat of hostile pagan tribes. It is important not to exaggerate the prevalence of learning and scholarship in monasteries from the fall of Rome up until the eleventh century. Nevertheless, many Christian monasteries became hubs of deep and wide learning, as well as preserving and copying manuscripts for later generations. In his *Institutes of Christian Culture* (562), Cassiodorus describes his monastery as a place where learning would be pursued. Both Christian and non-Christian Greek and Roman literature would be studied in monasteries modelled after Cassiodorus' ideal, with a basic curriculum mirroring what would eventually become the medieval university curriculum: arithmetic, music, geometry, astronomy, metaphysics, moral and political philosophy, economics, and, of course, theology.

Libraries were kept, books were copied, and literacy was passed down in monasteries around Europe. Many monasteries became hubs of learning where local children, particularly those of aristocrats, could expect to be educated in Latin. With expansionist campaigns undertaken by Charlemagne in the eighth and ninth centuries, monasteries were established around Western Europe, many of which harboured Charlemagne's appreciation of learning. Speaking of Charlemagne's court in Aachen, Peter Brown writes, 'the court acted as a "distribution centre" both for books and for personnel. Skilled and enthusiastic educators and administrators were drawn to the court and then were sent out to distant bishoprics and monasteries'. Thus, during the period leading up to the first universities in the late-eleventh century, learning and transmitting texts was kept alive, providing the scholarly materials for the institutionalisation of such learning in what would come to be known as the university.

Historian of the universities Walter Ruegg in his Preface to the multi-volume *History of the University in Europe*, summarises the intellectual spirit – the *amor sciendi* or love of knowing – of the early middle-ages into seven points, all of which became institutionalised in the university into the seventeenth century:

1. The belief in a world order created by God and open to rational investigation;
2. The ancient idea of the human being as an imperfect being; in Judaeo-Christian terms, a creature fallen into sin, and thus requiring instruction in morality and virtue;
3. Respect for the individual as bearing the image of God, and this being the foundation for the freedom to inquire into all forms of knowledge (*scientia* – where we get our word science);
4. The imperative to open truth claims to the basic norms of scientific and scholarly research and public disputation;
5. The recognition of knowledge as a gift from God and a public good whose value does not hinge on its economic potential;
6. Past learning is to be respected but also built upon and perfected;

knowledge progresses via a perpetual project of *reformation* (reformation); and

7. The equality and solidarity of scholars in the project of scientific-scholarly investigation.

The first university in the modern sense of the word was established at Bologna sometime in the later eleventh century (the exact date is unknown and there is no evidence to suggest it was 1088, the common date suggested). The university of Paris trailed by a few years.

Exactly how the first universities came into existence remains a matter of scholarly investigation, but it seems they emerged in towns in which teachers gathered over time to teach specific disciplines, law in the case of Bologna. From there these loose collections of teachers and students evolved into communities of learning and eventually were incorporated and declared *universitates*. According to Ruegg, 'The universal value of the quest for knowledge and of the transmission of knowledge, which has been recognised ever since antiquity, was thereby given an institutional setting in the university'.

The method of investigation taught and learned in the universities came to be known as scholasticism, which saw the best way of obtaining truth to be via the disciplines emphasised by Cassiodorus above. According to Edward Grant, 'it was in the esoteric domain of university scholasticism that reason was most highly developed and perhaps ultimately most influential'. It is true that initially at the University of Paris (est. 1150) lecturers were not permitted to teach – as opposed to read and discuss among the faculties – the metaphysics or natural philosophy of Aristotle. And yet by 1252 no student could take his bachelor's degree without having read Aristotle's logic and writings on the soul, and by 1255 Aristotle's *Physics*, *Metaphysics*, *De Animalibus* and his works on astronomy were to be read on the feast of John the Baptist.

Medieval scholars embraced Aristotle's empiricism such that science was institutionalised in the European university, ultimately culminating in the scientific revolution of the seventeenth century. Etienne Gilson said, 'We should deceive ourselves, however, if we credited the medieval with any love of science for science's sake… They turned towards nature because they were Christians… for what they saw and loved in it was nothing other than the work of God'.

The universities continued their traditions in Protestant Europe from the sixteenth century onwards. In America most of the most prominent universities were started by Christian denominations for the purposes of training the clergy or started with Christian goals explicit in their charters. The original 'Rules and Precepts' of Harvard University (est.1636) said 'Let every student be plainly instructed, and earnestly pressed to consider well, the main end of his life and studies is, to know God and Jesus Christ which is eternal life, John 17:3, and therefore to lay Christ in the bottom, as the only foundation of all sound knowledge and learning'. Harvard, Yale, Princeton, Brown, Columbia, and Rutgers all either started as denominational colleges or as explicitly Christian in goals. Alvin Schmitt in his *How Christianity Changed the World* says that prior to 1932 92% of all American Colleges and Universities were originally explicitly Christian institutions. Even the charter of the supposedly secular Sydney University (est.1850) saw the aims of the university as inculcating knowledge that is 'expedient for the better advancement of religion…'.

The modern university

The intellectual class of Europe became increasingly untethered from its orthodox Christianity especially from the mid-seventeenth century onwards. In the eighteenth-century deism – belief in a god but without revelation and miracles – was very common, and then atheism became increasingly common from the mid-nineteenth century onwards after Darwin's theory of natural selection was widely accepted. The universities

dechristianised well before the dechristianisation of the populations of
Europe, Australasia, and parts of America, especially from the 1960s
onwards. Into the universities crept the ideas of Karl Marx, Sigmund
Freud, and Friedrich Nietzsche – three architects of our intellectual age,
and each seeing their role as at least critiquing many of the premises of
Christian civilisation, even overturning it entirely. (Significant is that
Antonio Gramsci years earlier described socialism as the 'religion destined
to kill Christianity'.) As Carl Trueman shows in his remarkable history
of the modern mind *Triumph of the Modern Self*, the ideas of Marx,
Nietzsche, and Freud were integrated into twentieth century thought,
creating the doctrines of neo-Marxist and postmodern intellectuals that
would jostle for domination over humanities departments from the 1960s
to our own day.

Much as the traditional universities were supposed to form citizens
to continue the project of Christian civilisation, so the post-Christian
universities have adopted social engineering projects designed to erase
all vestiges of Christian civilisation. The American sociologist, C. Wright
Mills, set out the task of turning universities into mills of radicals in his
1960 *Letter to the New Left*. Mills dismissed working class radicalism as
'a legacy from Victorian Marxism that is now quite unrealistic'. More
hopeful were young intellectuals going through the post-WWII university
boom. Mills concluded by saying 'we've got to study these new generations
of intellectuals around the world as real live agencies of historic change'.
Similarly, the 1962 *Port Huron Statement* from Students for a Democratic
Society, the leading New Left society for student activism, saw universities
as 'an overlooked seat of influence'. The *Statement* went on to set out a
pretty clear agenda:

> *A new left must consist of younger people who matured in the post-
> war world, and partially be directed to the recruitment of younger
> people. The university is an obvious beginning point.*

An 'alliance of students and faculty' must 'wrest control of the educational process from the administrative bureaucracy... They must import major public issues into the curriculum... They must consciously *build a base* for their assault upon the loci of power'. I'd say the project was pretty successful. The radicalisation movement hit Australia in the early-1970s, most epitomised in the troubles at Sydney University between Marxist philosophers and traditional analytical philosophers, the latter objecting to the works of Chairman Mao, Che Gueverra, and other revolutionary writers being taught as serious philosophy. The philosophy department had an acrimonious split in 1973, all detailed in James Franklin's now-classic history of philosophy in Australia, *Corrupting the Youth.*

The leftist hegemony in the universities, humanities and education departments in particular, is no secret. A 2016 study of British academia produced by the Adam Smith Institute in London found that 'Around 50% of the general public supports right-wing or conservative parties, compared to less than 12% of academics'. A 2017 US study based on a sample of 5,197 tenure track academics from fifty-one of the sixty-six top ranked liberal arts colleges in the U.S. found that the Democratic-to-Republican ratio across the sample is 10.4:1.

In response to the Adam Smith Institute survey *The Conversation* – a left-leaning social commentary site for academics – published an article entitled 'Yes, academics tend to be left wing – but let's not exaggerate it'. Apologists of the leftist hegemony in universities argue that universities are not given to ideological balance; more specifically, to being well represented with conservatives. Universities will naturally attract left-leaning intellectuals. The fact that historically universities were well represented with conservatives until the 1960s, and universities themselves were frequently understood (and criticised) as conservative institutions, seems not to count for much in these ahistorical arguments.

The upshot is that academics are creating citizens in their own image. In 2016 the Pew Research Centre in the US produced a study showing that highly educated adults are far more likely than those with less education 'to take predominantly liberal [leftist] positions across a range of political values'. C. Wright Mills and the Students for a Democratic Society should be proud.

One of the most famous definitions of the high task of education comes from Matthew Arnold in his minor classic *Culture and Anarchy* (1869). The task is to pursue what Arnold calls 'culture', culture being 'a pursuit of our total perfection by means of getting to know, on all the matters which most concern us, the best which has been thought and said in the world, and, through this knowledge, turning a stream of fresh and free thought upon our stock notions and habits…'. An education ought to induct us into those thoughts which have something enduring and profound to say about human nature and the world in which we live. The most effective means of encountering 'the best which has been thought and said' is to study what we call the classic texts. I can think of no simpler or profound definition of a classic text than French historian Remi Brague's as 'a text from which one can always extract new ideas'.

Sadly, owing to the prevalence of Marxist and postmodern-inspired critical theories, the classic texts are often being marginalised or studied only to shed light on the injustices of the age from which the text sprung, or on our own age. Peter Wood in his remarkable book *Diversity: The Invention of a Concept*, says 'Diversity is probably the most powerful concept on American college campuses today'. Much the same can be said for British, Canadian, and Australasian campuses, and it is driven not simply by ideologues in humanities faculties, but by ideologues in university bureaucracies exploiting a sense of victimhood that animates our age as well as the pusillanimity of university leaders to speak out against it.

Let us consider an example listed by Heather Mac Donald in *The Diversity Delusion: How Race and Gender Pandering Corrupt the University and Undermine Our Culture*. At the University of California, Los Angeles up to 2011 it was compulsory for students majoring in English literature to take one course in Chaucer, two in Shakespeare, and one in Milton. Following a push by the younger academics, this was scrapped and replaced with a requirement to take a total of three courses from among the following four areas:

1. Gender, Race, Ethnicity, Disability, and Sexuality Studies
2. Imperial, Transnational, and Postcolonial Studies
3. Genre Studies, Interdisciplinary Studies, and Critical Theory
4. Creative Writing

In other words, the English major became nominally indifferent to whether students had a deep understanding of the classic texts and cared more about students' ability to interpret text via the lens of critical race, sexuality, and other studies; or what Helen Pluckrose and James Lindsay in their *Cynical Theories* called 'grievance studies'. In the Australian context many scholars have critiqued the state of Australian universities, humanities departments in particular. *Quadrant Magazine* is an excellent repository of thoughtful critique by perceptive commentators including John Carroll, Pierre Ryckmans, Merv Bendel, Kevin Donnelly, and Keith Windschuttle among others. Gregory Melleuish's book *Australian Intellectuals: Their Strange History and Pathological Tendencies* is also illuminating. Although not focussing on Australia, the Australian-born *Quillette* has been invaluable in terms of offering insightful critiques of the state of the university internationally.

It is an exaggeration to say that the classic texts are no longer studied in universities. It is more accurate to say that texts in universities and high schools are frequently studied not to be mined for what they can tell us about the true, beautiful, the good, and the virtuous, but for what they can teach us about racial, sexual, and gender oppression. As Scruton says, 'Studies in the humanities are now designed to prove... the culture of the West has no deeper meaning than the power that it served to perpetuate... The university, instead of transmitting culture, exists to deconstruct it, to remove its "aura", and to leave the student, after four years of intellectual dissipation, with the view that anything goes and nothing matters'.

We should be careful not to suggest that the greatest problems with the universities are owing to leftist ideology. The universities have become overly utilitarian and corporatised since the 1980s, particularly in Australia, but the trend is global. As Scruton says, 'the curriculum centers not on sublime and purposeless subjects like ancient Greek... but on sciences, vocational disciplines, and the now ubiquitous "business studies"'. Universities, no longer lavishly funded by governments, scramble for money from vocational degrees and Masters programmes, not to mention appealing to the rising middle classes in China and India. The rise of international students has inevitably led to a decline in standards owing to the often lower level of English proficiency among international students. Students don't travel from across the globe and pay tens of thousands of dollars up front to fail essays and examinations, and universities know it.

Another problem with the modern university is that for decades it is not really been a university at all, rather a multiversity: a collection of discrete disciplines that rarely meet anymore, at least at the faculty level. It was not meant to be this way. John Henry Newman in his *Idea of a University* said 'all Knowledge is a whole and the separate sciences parts of one... Hence it is that the Sciences, into which our knowledge may be said to be cast, have multiplied one on another, and an internal sympathy, and admit, or rather demand, comparison and adjustment'. In other words, all the disciplines—if they render knowledge—complement one another. Perhaps we have forgotten this, at least practically, and perhaps the consequences for the humanities are clear: subjectivism, emotivism, rank denial of brute facts to which even the humanities should be held accountable.

Are the sciences and the humanities in any kind of dialogue, as they were in the medieval model? What could the sciences learn from the humanities, and vice versa? Well for one thing, the humanities could learn that there is such a thing as objective reality, facts, and a world independent of our language and of our feelings. This is central to the sciences but has been challenged relentlessly by certain humanities disciplines now for forty years.

Take some typical prose of Judith Butler, queer theorist and birth-parent of modern transgender ideology. This from her book *Gender Trouble*, a book that all but outright rejects the objectivity of sex altogether:

> *Are the ostensibly natural facts of sex discursively produced by various scientific discourses in the service of other political and social interests? If the immutable character of sex is contested, perhaps this construct called 'sex' is as culturally constructed as gender…*

Now any biologist would find the idea that binary sex – outside of very rare circumstances – is not an objective fact grounded in objective reality very strange indeed. But this very idea suffuses humanities departments and students.

It is common for representatives of the humanities to glibly chide the representatives of the sciences, the former chiding the latter for having no understanding beyond their test tubes and mathematical formulae. In reality, given the impact of critical theories that have emerged out of humanities and sociology departments, not to mention the transgender movement itself, I think the representatives of the sciences have just as much cause to be glib about the state of the humanities. If the scientists could learn a thing or two about culture and ideas from the humanities, the humanities could stand to relearn that there are some things that just are, and even the humanities need to submit to the tribunal of facts, reality, and, when appropriate, testability.

The way forward

As Frank Furedi shows in his *What's Happened to the University?* universities have become increasingly hostile to freedom of speech and increasingly censorious of speech and ideas deemed 'harmful' and 'unsafe'– 'harmful' and 'unsafe' the new ways of saying 'heresy' in an increasingly therapeutic, mental health-preoccupied society. This is the part of the essay where readers may expect me to issue a rallying cry to reform the universities. Maybe such reform is possible, but it's doubtful. The rot has set in and the odd conservative-culturalist that sneaks into a humanities faculty usually makes little to no impact on the overall character of the department. Indeed, the most vocal critics of cancel culture in the universities are left-leaning intellectuals who as a class exorcised universities of conservatives over the last fifty years. Even if the identity politics radicals in the universities were neutered by their tenured critics, all that would result is the resumption of left-dominated faculties, not faculties with genuine viewpoint diversity.

Scruton reminds us 'The most precious gift of our civilization, and the one that was most under threat during the twentieth century, is the freedom to associate'. The upshot for Scruton is that as long as this freedom exists, 'the fact that we can no longer entrust our high culture to the universities matters less'. In other words, the time has come to speak less about reforming the universities and more about alternative institutions and arrangements for the transmission of learning and culture.

We must remember that today's great universities all started off as small institutions, often privately funded – certainly in America that is the case. This will be easier in some countries than in others. America already has set a good precedent, and one wonders what the potential to do this in the UK may be. There are hopeful signs in Australia at the moment with Campion College – currently Australia's greatest embodiment of a liberal arts college – in Sydney going from strength to strength. The Ramsay Centre for Western Civilisation is also doing good things, although it faces the challenge of its own goals having to negotiate with hostility towards those goals within the universities in which their programs are run. There is also the newly established Emmanuel College in Sydney, a Protestant liberal arts college, as well as many theological colleges that could increasingly introduce broader liberal arts subjects. Alphacrucis College, that recently won registration as a university college, is another example all is not lost.

Also, as is the practice in America, philanthropists in Britain and Australasia need to get on board with the long-term project of cultural restoration and fund not only new institutions or independent centres in existing institutions – as long as those centres, like other centres in these institutions, can remain consistent with their values – but also set up sinecures or stipends for Christian and culturally conservative scholars who have no hope of getting tenured positions in the universities. To speak briefly of left and right, universities effectively offer sinecures to thousands of leftist scholars who spend a lot of time teaching the youth and producing work that will continue to undermine many of the ideals that have made Western societies so worthy. Without the help of philanthropists the best conservative minds will be wasted and of no impact in the culture wars.

One final note on virtual learning. There may be worth in recalling that a degree and an education are not synonymous, and a person can become well educated without setting foot in a bricks and mortar university, or even without taking a degree. With the rise of the internet there has appeared an abundance of high-quality information in print and lecture form, most of which is free, for anyone to access. Lately this writer has been slowly working through the American philosopher John Searle's UCLA Berkeley lectures on the philosophy of language posted on YouTube – freely available to anyone. Much as the rise of the printing press and the rise of cheap editions of classic literature made a well-rounded mind possible for the average homemaker and tradesman, so the rise of the internet provides teaching materials and texts from the greatest minds of history, and today's greatest teachers. Merely sitting down with pen and paper and working through the lectures of Sir Roger Scruton, not to mention hundreds of university course lectures on various topics, will go a long way to sharpening and expanding one's own mind. YouTube and other online sites could prove to be an excellent way for untenured scholars and experts to get their ideas heard and create followers. I expect the material to improve even more over time. The one drawback, I must say, is that without assessment tasks, it could be harder to retain knowledge. But then again, submitting assessed work makes up only three to four years of one's life of education, the rest being autodidactic anyway.

I am not saying that the universities are a lost cause, but I am saying that they have proven so recalcitrant to reform that it is time to change strategy and to start again, not from scratch, but upon the worthy example set by the universities of the Western tradition since the classical period, and most spectacularly from the medieval period onwards. The state of the universities could be seen as a crisis, but also as an opportunity for a new age of cultural pioneers whose declining faith in the universities is accompanied by a bold faith in the blessings of Christianity, and the gift to wider society that a renewal of Christian education, particularly tertiary education, would be.

Dr. Stephen Chavura, Ph.D., teaches European and Australian history at Campion College, Sydney. Before he worked at Campion he was a lecturer in sociology and political philosophy at various Australian universities. He has published in numerous journals including History of European Ideas, Journal of Religious History, *and* Australian Journal of Political Science. *His most recent (co-authored) books are* The Forgotten Menzies: The Mind of Australia's Longest-Serving Prime Minister *(2021), and* Reason, Religion, and the Australian Polity: A Secular State? *(2019). He also writes opinion pieces on current affairs that have appeared in* The Australian, Spectator Australia, *and* ABC Religion and Ethics.

The Challenge of Preserving Catholic Education in a Post-Christian Society

Stephen Elder

Catholic schools enrol approximately 20 per cent of students across Australia and research proves such schools, except for selective state schools, outperform government schools in Year 12 results and tertiary entry, plus encouraging volunteerism and social capital. At the same time and not withstanding their popularity, Catholic schools, and faith-based schools in general, are increasingly challenged by a radical secular curriculum promoting woke ideology.

As argued by critics including the historian Geoffrey Blainey and the Melbourne based Institute of Public Affairs, the 2021 revised Australian national curriculum, and state based equivalent documents, fail to properly acknowledge Western civilisation's debt to Judeo-Christianity. The situation is made more difficult given we are living in a post-Christian age; an age where religion is devalued and where materialism, self-centredness and a utilitarian view of life prevail. The challenge faced by Catholic schools is how to respond and how best to remain true to their teachings and their faith. The first step is to understand the nature of the threat.

The Leftist 'Long March'

Workers of all countries unite; you have nothing to lose but your chains!

This slogan appears both in *The Communist Manifesto* and as an inscription on the tombstone of Karl Marx in London. It reflects Marxist theory that the class-based resentments generated by the contradictions of capitalism would unify working people across borders in armed revolt against bourgeois democracy. The so-called proletarian revolution was supposed to be inexorable and inevitable.

Then came July 1914.

Socialist intellectuals were appalled by the sight of French, German, Russian, Austrian and British young men flocking to their national colours by the millions. It turned out that patriotism was a far more potent force than socialism when the call to enlist or mobilise was heard.

After the war Marxist theorists set their minds to rationalising why they got things so wrong. And the most enduring of those rationalisations is presented in the *Selections from the Prison Notebooks* written by an Italian communist named Antonio Gramsci.

Gramsci argues capitalist, free-market democracies prosper and survive not merely because of their monopoly on armed force, but also because they dominant the cultural norms that serve as a bulwark against Marxist revolution. He was particularly impressed by the ability of the Catholic Church to satisfy the spiritual needs of people within the framework of existing political and economic systems. Not surprisingly Gramsci describes socialism as the 'religion destined to kill Christianity'.

The so-called 'cultural hegemony' of traditional Christianity and free-market capitalism must be destroyed if communism is to triumph. It was Gramsci's belief that Marxism must create an alternative system of faith that will fulfil the spiritual yearnings that are part of the human condition.

Fast forward 40 years to 1968, when the Western world was swept by a wave of popular discontent directed against the traditional political and social order. From Paris to Sydney and Chicago to Berlin, hordes of young Leftists took to the streets in protests that were sometimes violent. In Europe, this generation of twenty-something student protesters became known as 'soixant huitards,' a French term that translates as '68ers'.

One of the leading soixant huitards was Rudy 'the Red' Deutschke, a German student activist. Deutschke was raised in a pious Lutheran home and incorporated that same evangelistic fervour to Marxism, writing that Jesus Christ was the greatest political revolutionary in history.

It was Deutschke who built upon the ideas of Gramsci to propose that the Left must embark on a 'long march through the institutions of power' in order to subvert free-market democracy from within.

In his 1972 book *Counterrevolution and Revolt*, Marxist philosopher Herbert Marcuse wrote:

> *Rudi Deutschke has proposed the strategy of the long march through the institutions: working against the established institutions while working within them, but not simply by 'boring from within', rather by 'doing the job', learning (how to program and read computers, how to teach at all levels of education, how to use the mass media, how to organize production, how to recognize and eschew planned obsolescence, how to design, et cetera), and at the same time preserving one's own consciousness in working with others.*

Now a half-century later, the results of the long march are evident throughout Western societies, including Australia. It began with the universities, where the faculties of arts, social sciences and education evolved into Leftist monocultures where progressivism reigns supreme.

American surveys of faculty political orientation reveal how stark the dominance of the Left has become within higher education. A report of university faculty political affiliation published in 2016 found that the ratio of registered Democrats to Republicans within history departments was 33-to-1. In faculties of journalism, the Democrat-to-Republican ratio was 20-to-1, while in law schools it was 8.6-to-1. The least imbalanced academic discipline was economics, where the ratio was 4.5 Democrats to every single Republican.

In his September 2021 resignation letter from Portland State University, philosopher Peter Boghossian details how the long march has corrupted American tertiary education:

> *I never once believed – nor do I believe now – that the purpose*
> *of instruction was to lead my students to a particular conclusion.*
> *Rather, I sought to create the conditions for rigorous thought; to help*
> *them gain the tools to hunt and furrow for their own conclusions...*
> *But brick by brick, the university has made this kind of intellectual*
> *exploration impossible. It has transformed a bastion of free inquiry*
> *into a Social Justice factory whose only inputs were race, gender, and*
> *victimhood and whose only outputs were grievance and division.*

Anyone who has passed through an Australian university over recent decades knows that here the situation is no different. Case in point is the physics Professor Peter Ridd, who was sacked by James Cook University because of statements to the media and articles in a peer-reviewed scientific journal criticising the environmental radicalism of certain other academics. Ridd's crime was to question the prevailing left narrative that global warming was destroying the Great Barrier Reef.

This Leftist lock on higher education has served as a vector through which so-called 'woke' ideologies have percolated through Australian society. Our universities are where Australia's intellectual elites are educated and credentialed. Our lawyers, journalists and managerial class are all too often moulded by their higher education experience.

University schools of education have been the most dangerous disseminators of Leftist dogma. For years they have been churning out woke graduates who've been taught to view our national history and culture through a warped politicised prism that highlights the negative while obscuring the positive. What the great historian Geoffrey Blainey describes as a 'black armband' view of Australian history.

While most of today's teachers have never read a single word written by Karl Marx, the reality is they have been indoctrinated in post-modern critical theory that revolves around an attitude set forth by Marx in 1843:

It is all the more clear what we have to accomplish at present: I am referring to ruthless criticism of all that exists.

Oikophobia and The 'Great Awokening'

The late British cultural critic Roger Scruton uses the term 'oikophobia' to describe today's woke ideology that can be traced to Marxist theory that originated with the publication of Das Kapital over 154 years ago. Created by a fusion of the Greek words for household and fear, Scruton defines oikophobia as:

> ... a peculiar frame of mind that has arisen throughout the Western world since the Second World War, and which is particularly prevalent among the intellectual and political élites. No adequate word exists for this attitude, though its symptoms are instantly recognised: namely, the disposition, in any conflict, to side with 'them' against 'us', and the felt need to denigrate the customs, culture and institutions that are identifiably 'ours'... Oikophobia is a stage through which the adolescent mind normally passes. But it is a stage in which some people – intellectuals especially – tend to become arrested. As George Orwell pointed out, intellectuals on the Left are especially prone to it, and this has often made them willing agents of foreign powers.

A draft new national curriculum published early 2021 by the Australian Curriculum Assessment and Reporting Authority (ACARA), reflects the extent to which the oikophobic rot has spread through our educational establishment.

The draft was so bad that federal education minister Alan Tudge
sent ACARA back to the drawing board, rejecting the proposed history
curriculum on the grounds it:

> ... diminishes Australia's western, liberal, and democratic
> values. The overarching impression from the curriculum is that the
> main feature of western civilisation is slavery, imperialism and
> colonisation. Important historical events are removed or reframed,
> such as the emphasis on invasion theory over Australia Day. Even
> Anzac Day is presented as a contested idea, rather than the most
> sacred of all days where we honour the millions of men and women
> who have served in war, and the 100,000 who gave their lives for
> our freedom.

A propensity to see people as a member of collectives rather than
as individuals is a pillar of the Leftist worldview. In classical Marxism
this group identity revolves around economic class. But since the
end of the Cold War the Leftist 'ruthless criticism of all that exists'
has metastasised into an obsessive focus on identity politics and
victimhood described as intersectionality.

Intersectional theory categorises people according to the minority
group to which they claim membership and the degree of historic
oppression that group has suffered. This doctrine generates what theorist
Patricia May Collins describes as a 'matrix of domination' that assigns
virtue or vice by 'intersectional' categories of race, ethnicity and sexual
group identity. Based on this theory anyone who celebrates and defends
Western civilisation and Judeo-Christianity is condemned as Eurocentric
and guilty of white supremacism.

Membership in a woke minority group confers social prestige
and immunity to criticism so long as there is no deviation from
intersectional dogma. And because this status also delivers advantages
in employment, education and other government benefits, intersectional

theory has spawned an ugly form of competitive victimology in which people compete for the title of most oppressed. Writer Matt Yglesias coined the semi-tongue-in-cheek phrase the 'great awokening' to describe this phenomenon.

'Woke' and Catholic are Incompatible

The antipathy towards religious faith that permeates Leftist thought can, of course, be traced back to Karl Marx, who famously derided religion as the 'opium of the masses'. As we have seen, during the 1920s Italian communist Antonio Gramsci described the Catholic Church as a powerful opponent that should be emulated and, if possible, subverted from within. And over the past century, certain fringe elements of our Church have succumbed to the siren song of Leftist thought.

Without wishing to engage in a grand theological inquiry, I will assert the self-evident truth that Catholicism and Leftist politics are antithetical. In my view there are two insurmountable reasons why wokism and the Catholic faith are incompatible—collectivism and coercion.

I have already mentioned the Leftist insistence on defining people, not as individuals endowed with distinct human dignity by the grace of God, but first and foremost as members of a collective. This is contrary to the teachings of our Catechism in which the sacraments of salvation confer a state of grace to individual people depending on their faith disposition. In our Catholic faith, the relationship with God is intensely personal and individual. God created each person in his image and endowed each individual with the power of free thought and free will.

And then there's the issue of coercion. Care for the poor has been an essential tenet of the Christian tradition since the Gospels first relayed the story of Jesus during the 1st century AD. Yet while 'caritas' (the Latin for charity) has been encouraged by our Church in word and in deed for two millennia, the act of almsgiving has always been the result of a voluntary choice.

By contrast, Leftist policy agendas invariably revolve around the forcible redistribution of wealth. Whether it be the seizure of private property under classical Marxism or the sky-high taxation rates imposed by Scandinavian nations to fund their expansive welfare-state systems, these policies rely on the police power of the state for their enforcement.

Yet the Catholic Church believes acts imposed by the threat of physical coercion attract neither spiritual nor moral merit. There is nothing virtuous about paying one's tax debt when the alternative is criminal prosecution by government.

The Leftist penchant for coercion becomes even more problematic when applied to the realms of the family and marriage. While the Catholic principle of 'reject the sin, accept the sinner' mandates a loving attitude towards all of humanity, the Church continues to stand by its biblical doctrines of faith. And this stance places Catholicism in direct opposition to essential elements of the worldview espoused by the modern Left.

One might think that this shouldn't constitute a problem in our liberal democracy. After all, freedom of conscience and religious practice have been pillars of our free political system. And the principle of live and let live should allow progressives to conduct their lives as they see fit, while persons of traditional religious faith do the same.

Fine in theory, except for the fact that Leftists are positively enthusiastic about using the police power of the state as a cudgel to impose their view of the world upon all. During the marriage referendum campaign, the Australian Marriage Equality lobby group advocated for the complete repeal of all religious exemptions in Australian anti-discrimination law. Another advocacy group, Equality Australia, sought to 'narrow all exemptions for faith-based organisations'.

If these proposals are enacted into law, persons of traditional Christian belief will be threatened with legal sanctions for adhering to a biblical perspective on marriage and family.

The Challenge of Ensuring that Catholic schools remain Catholic

Like most Western nations, Australia's dominant culture today is post-Christian. This assertion is borne out by census figures that reveal Australians professing Christian beliefs declined from 88.2 per cent of the population in 1966 to 52.1 per cent in 2016.

And as we have seen, the clash between the woke culture of post-Christian Australia and Catholic religious doctrine creates a conundrum for Catholic education.

By definition, our schools operate according to a Christ-centred set of values that promote the intellectual, spiritual, emotional and physical growth of our students. We present Jesus as a role model to build a culture of compassion and caring that complements our emphasis on academic excellence. It is this holistic fusion of the spiritual and academic that sets Catholic and other faith-based schools apart.

Our teachers are an indispensable part of this equation. They are the front-line staff who serve as essential conduits through which academic excellence is fostered and Christian values and virtues are transmitted to our students. Our teachers are a precious resource that must be nourished and cherished. Yet in order to ensure that Catholic schools convey distinctly Catholic values, we must be able to select staff who subscribe to the tenets of our religious tradition. This principle must apply, not only to those who teach explicitly religious subjects, but to teachers of maths, English, science and history as well. Teachers are not only educators, but role models as well. And in order to create an explicitly Catholic educational environment, the explicit and implicit example set by staff must conform to Catholic religious teaching.

Yet, this principle of religious autonomy is currently under threat by progressive governments that vow to make it illegal for faith-based schools to select staff on the basis of adherence to religious tradition.

If this eventuates, Christian schools will be forced to employ staff who

THE CHALLENGE OF PRESERVING CATHOLIC EDUCATION

openly spurn Christian religious teaching. This would threaten to dilute the Catholic essence of our schools to the point where they become CINO—Catholic in name only. CINO-ism will be the kiss of death for Catholic education, which in turn will create a serious danger to the intergenerational health of our Church.

After all, why would parents pay to have their children attend schools that simply affix a pseudo-Christian façade to the same secular values that are offered by the tuition-free state school just down the street? Sentiments of alumni loyalty and solid test scores will not be enough.

If the sole distinction between Catholic schools and their state counterparts becomes the Latin lettering on their coats of arms, Catholic schools will wither on the proverbial vine. In order to thrive over the long term, Catholic schools must offer a vibrant faith-based alternative to the extreme secularity of Australian culture. Without apology, or hesitation, we must ensure that our Catholic schools remain true to Catholic teaching and faith traditions.

Recent events in the United States provide a salutary example how this can be done through parental pressure at the local level. From California to Virginia and from Minnesota to Florida, local school boards are facing spontaneous eruptions of grass-roots protest by parents outraged over the introduction of leftist dogma into their children's classrooms. Parents have been especially angered by critical race theory being forced on students, a neo-Marxist inspired theory where whiteness is condemned and American society is attacked as structurally racist.

Over recent months YouTube has been filled with remarkable video clips of impassioned mothers and fathers queuing for hours to speak against efforts by Leftist educational bureaucrats to indoctrinate children in Leftist dogma. When investigative journalists exposed an Antifa activist teacher whose professed aim was to turn his students into revolutionaries, indignant parents forced the school district in California to sack him.

This non-violent parental uprising that we see emerging in the United States is heartening and also instructive. What American fathers and mothers are doing can be done here in Australia as well.

Having run Australia's largest Catholic education system for 17 years, I can attest that there was no way I could be aware of everything that was happening on a daily basis at each of the 300-plus schools under my guidance. But Australian Catholic parents can follow the example of their American counterparts. They must keep their fingers on the pulse of what is being taught to their children in the classroom. And if untoward indoctrination occurs, mothers and fathers, aunts and uncles and grandparents should speak up in protest without fear or hesitation. Parents should mobilise to make their voices heard so loudly that they cannot be ignored.

The future of our schools and our faith depends on it.

Stephen Elder has enjoyed a distinguished career in both Government and education. This includes being a member of the Victorian Legislative Assembly from 1988 to 1999 and acting as the Parliamentary Secretary for Education responsible for the Government's reform agenda in Education from 1988 to 1999. Mr Elder was the Executive Director of Catholic Education for the Archdiocese of Melbourne from 2006 to 2018 and other positions include being on the Senate of Australian Catholic University, Executive Director of the Catholic Education Commission of Victoria, member of the National Catholic Education Commission, Secretary of Catholic Capital Grants, Director of the Australian Institute for Teaching and School Leadership and being appointed to the Board of the Victorian Registration and Qualifications Authority. In 2016 Stephen was awarded a Medal of the Order of Australia for service to the Catholic Church in Australia and to the community of Victoria. In 2018 he was ranked first in the Australian Financial Review's *list of the five most powerful people in education.*

Health and Social Welfare

Tim Costello

Early Christians risked persecution and death to advocate justice for all. They established the first public hospitals and hospices for anyone in need, regardless of their status. They stood up for the rights of the vulnerable. Not for political gain, but because they were inspired by something greater. In the Gospels as well as Acts, we see Christians ministering to the vulnerable and marginalised, even challenging societal structures that weighed down upon them.

Revolutionary Christians with a passion for healthcare and social justice have come from a variety of political spectrums. What they have in common is the belief that change comes through understanding God, not through any political or social machinations. It was the Christian belief, drawing on the Old and New Testaments, that human rights have their origin in creation and a covenant that proclaims all humans have value and are deserving of dignity and care.

Historically, many great social movements have their roots within faith communities – from campaigning against slavery and child labour, to modern civil rights, anti-apartheid roles in South Africa and now the climate change debates. Faith has been the fuel that has fed the passionate quest for social justice and animated many movements for social reform. The US civil rights campaign, for example, led by Martin Luther King, was largely influenced by Christians. Indeed it must be faith that influences politics, not the reverse. When politics influences faith it is politicised and controversial.

American author Peter Wehner wrote that many Christians have embraced the worst aspects of culture and politics. While acknowledging the 'countless acts of kindness, generosity, and self-giving love' performed every day by Christians, he asks: 'How is it that evangelical Christianity has become, for too many of its adherents, a political religion? When the Christian faith is politicised, churches become repositories not of grace but of grievances, places where tribal identities are reinforced, where fears are nurtured, and where aggression and nastiness are sacralised'.

Our Creator is revealed through Christianity as the God of the downtrodden and suffering. He requires us to stand firmly against injustice. It is not just a religious theory, it is the business of humanity; not a luxury but a necessity.

In Matthew 25, Jesus's parable instructs His followers to care for the hungry, thirsty, homeless, naked, sick, and imprisoned – the marginalised, in whom His face can be revealed. The imagery is powerful as Jesus commands us to care for 'the least of these'. Who are the most marginalised in society other than the sick, the elderly, the homeless, the prisoners, the deprived children? In them we see the face of Christ.

The rise of Christianity, according to many historians, was because the early Christians were widely known for their love for each other and their neighbours. That was counter intuitive because at the time justice demanded that everyone got what they deserved. Mercy, grace and love shown by the Christians were uncharacteristic in the brutal and often inhumane ancient world. It was a 'user pays' society. The weak and the sick were despised. Abortion, infanticide and poisoning were widely practised, even by so-called doctors.

Author and theologian Timothy Keller said the early church was strikingly different from the culture around it. He said: 'The pagan society was stingy with its money and promiscuous with its body. A pagan gave nobody their money and practically gave everybody their body. And the Christians came along and gave practically nobody their body and they gave practically everybody their money'.

Christian communities became known as places where people tended to live longer and healthier lives, because when they suffered sickness, poverty or mishap there were Christians who provided for their need. And Christians extended love way beyond the boundaries of family and congregation to their pagan neighbours. Like the Good Samaritan, they advanced the concept of caring for a neighbour beyond casual acquaintance to genuine service. Jesus' definition of neighbour was anyone God brings across our path.

The historian Henry Chadwick records that in 251 A.D., a great plague struck the Greco-Roman world. Memories were revived of a plague a century earlier in which more than a third of the population died. Fear was everywhere. Those who could afford it fled to the countryside. Those who could not remained in the cities. When they went to the temples they found them empty, the priests having fled. Pagan households threw sufferers onto the streets and cities were filled with those who had become infected.

But Christian communities, according to Henry Chadwick, took an entirely different approach. They saw it as their responsibility to love the sick and dying, so they took them into their own homes and nursed them. This action meant that many people recovered who otherwise would have died. Historians suggest that elementary nursing could have reduced the mortality rate by as much as two thirds, but it also cost a number of Christian carers their lives.

The practical application of charity and sacrifice was probably the most potent single cause of Christian success in the early years. The prolific second century writer Tertullian reported that Christian acts of compassion to the wider world astonished the pagans. He said the words 'See how these Christians love one another' was the continual cry of the pagans.

When the Roman Emperor Constantine endorsed Christianity in the 4th century, the church set up burial societies, poorhouses, homes for the aged, shelter for the homeless, hospitals, and orphanages. A later ruler, Julian, was the last Roman Emperor who tried to reinstitute paganism. In his Apology, Julian said that if the old religion wanted to succeed, it would need to care for people even better than the way Christians cared.

The early Christians saw everyone as a child of God. They proclaimed that God loves everyone. So we see that social welfare and justice for all is in our DNA as Christians.

Tom Holland's book *Dominion: The Making of The Western Mind* explores the grand thesis that our modern Western values and ethics are utterly saturated by and grounded in Christian concepts. He states that the West, despite efforts to distance itself from religion, remains firmly moored to its Christian past. Christianity may be the most enduring and influential legacy of the ancient world, and its emergence the single most transformative development in Western history. In Holland's view, even Karl Marx saw history as a battleground between cosmic forces of good and evil.

Holland states the impact of Christianity has been so profound on the development of Western civilisation that it has come to be hidden from view. This is a blind spot in contemporary culture. The secularists, even those who have a disdain for Christian faith, might claim the Enlightenment invented the good values of today – including forgiveness, humility and care for the poor and weak. But unbeknown to themselves they are judging through a Christian lens.

Holland's view is that progressives and conservatives are bred from the same moral matrix. Therefore, the climate change protests, Woke and

Black Lives Matter movements could well be defined as a continuation of the restless ethos that a light shining in the darkness can change the world. Whether we acknowledge it or not, we are all heirs to the Christian revolution. Even the prominent atheist Richard Dawkins has described himself as a 'secular Christian'. As Sydney Anglican Peter Jensen says we are secular 'in a Christian sort of way'.

An Ipsos poll conducted across 23 countries in 2017 found that 49 per cent of adults thought religion does more harm than good in the world. A higher proportion of Australians polled – 63 per cent – agreed that we'd be better off without religion. But 71 per cent recognised that Christians had a positive effect in the charity and social welfare sector. Australians most valued the work of Christian organisations for looking after the homeless, for offering financial assistance/food relief programs and providing disaster relief.

Interestingly, in a 2018 McCrindle survey, nearly 1.5 million Australian adults said they did not know any Christians at all. For those who knew at least one Christian, the top words used to describe Christians were caring, loving and kind. Most Australians surveyed said they valued Christians for their work with the needy. So, although many do not personally know any Christians, they appreciate their value in society.

Australians are often not attracted to the idea of church or to the church as an institution. They are sceptical about outward displays of piety or of anything that smacks of hypocrisy. Many Australians will never darken a church door by choice. And yet they thank God for the Salvos and their other Christian counterparts.

Christianity played a key role in the development of the Australian colony and consequently, the Judeo-Christian ethic is still part of the Australian identity. Christians throughout our nation's history established hospitals, schools, churches, aged-care facilities, and many welfare agencies.

Historian Geoffrey Blainey, in his book *A Shorter History of Australia*, said that the Christian churches did 'more than any other institution, public or private, to civilise Australians'.

In his address to the Catholic World Youth Day 2008 in Sydney, then-prime minister Kevin Rudd said that Christianity had been an overwhelming force for good in Australia. He said: 'It was the church that began first schools for the poor, it was the church that began first hospitals for the poor, it was the church that began first refuges for the poor and these great traditions continue for the future'. In 2012, the non-religious then-prime minister Julia Gillard praised the historical welfare work of the Salvation Army in Australia as 'Christianity with its sleeves rolled up'. Gillard also stressed the value of the Bible, arguing it 'formed such an important part of our culture' and that 'it is impossible to understand Western literature without that key of understanding the Bible stories and how Western literature builds on them'.

Research by the Federal Government found Australians who attend church are more likely to donate their time and money to the community, contributing almost half a billion dollars to the economy. A 2018 report, titled 'Donating and Volunteering Behaviour Associated with Religiosity' conducted by Deloitte Access Economics, found that people who do not attend church as children but start attending religious services as adults are 1.7 times more likely to be a volunteer – and 1.5 times more likely to make donations – compared with those who have never attended religious services.

The wellbeing of the poor and vulnerable was a vital part of the Christian mission during the earliest period of colonial settlement in Australia. Their grounding in evangelical Christianity made their involvement in bodily care an intrinsic part of their role. That ethos was welcomed, and relied upon, by colonial administrations as a cost-effective way to remove the burdens of government bureaucracy.

Christian charitable organisations, hospitals and schools have played a prominent role in welfare and education since colonial times, when the First Fleet's Church of England chaplain, Richard Johnson, was credited as 'the physician both of soul and body' during the famine of 1790. At the time, a convict wrote home:

> I believe few of the sick would recover if it was not for the kindness of the Rev Mr Johnson, whose assistance out of his own stores makes him the physician both of soul and body, as he laboured in all the ways he knew how to care for the colony's sick and poor, to assist in the best farming practises, to run all the schooling, to conduct hundreds of baptisms, marriages, and funerals, and to preach the central message of the Christian faith, all the while refusing to play the role of 'moral policeman'.

Johnson became our nation's first carer for orphans and the indigenous. John Newton, the evangelical who wrote the hymn Amazing Grace, gave Johnson the title 'Patriarch of the Southern Hemisphere'.

Historian Stuart Piggin said evangelical Christianity was 'an intense, vital personal religion' that greatly influenced the colonial public sphere by the end of the eighteenth century. The evangelicals believed charity was incomplete without the pursuit of justice. Piggin said: 'It's primarily a lay movement and, therefore, the public side of it is very important. It is concerned about lay concerns like education, health, politics and trade unions, all those sorts of things'.

John Saunders, one of Australia's first Baptist pastors, developed schools, welcomed migrants, organised charities and opposed convict transportation. In a landmark sermon, Rev Saunders argued for indigenous rights and the recognition of Aboriginal humanity, drawing a distinction between 'pity' and 'justice'.

Around the same time, the British House of Commons Select Committee on Aborigines, heavily influenced by evangelical concepts, acknowledged that: '...the native inhabitants of any land have an incontrovertible right to their own soil; a plain and sacred right, however which seems not to be understood'. Britain's Colonial Secretary, Lord Glenelg, and his Under Secretary James Stephen, both members of the evangelical Christian philanthropists called the Clapham Sect, ordered that Aboriginal land rights be upheld and that no land be taken over where Aboriginal title exists. But colonial commissioners were determined to protect the colonial economy. While they tacitly agreed to protect Aborigines from violence and to provide subsistence, shelter, education and Christian teaching, they took steps to ensure that all land was available for sale regardless of Aboriginal ownership and occupation.

The NSW Benevolent Society was our nation's first official charity. Founded in 1813, and originally known as The NSW Society for Promoting Christian Knowledge and Benevolence, it aimed 'to relieve the poor, the distressed, the aged, the infirm, to discourage begging and to encourage industrious habits among the poor and to provide them with religious instruction'. It was soon active in emergency relief, in the form of food provision to supplement the insufficient government rations. It was the first private charitable organisation dedicated to meeting needs of vulnerable groups in Australian society, assisting people far beyond the capacity of government.

Governor Lachlan Macquarie became a regular donor. The Society provided cash loans, grants, food and clothing, set up a refuge for homeless older men, deserted women and children and the mentally ill and was the first to introduce district nursing to care for those who were isolated. It also established the colony's first maternity hospital.

In 1838, the first Sisters of Charity arrived in Australia offering care to female prisoners in Parramatta. The first Roman Catholic Orphan School was established at Parramatta in the 1840s. An orphanage in Adelaide was among the first works of Mary Mackillop's Sisters of St Joseph.

Catholic laywoman Caroline Chisholm responded to the plight of young immigrant and homeless women in 1840s Sydney. Her employment agency found safe jobs for many in city and rural areas and her immigration scheme brought many more to the colony.

In 1854, the St Vincent de Paul Society was set up to address the increased number of homeless and deserted children roaming the streets. St Vincent's Hospital Sydney was founded in 1857. St Vincent's Melbourne was founded in 1893. From these modest beginnings a significant network of health services, schools, social agencies and advocates were established along the eastern seaboard of Australia.

In 1883, Salvation Army Officers provided accommodation and support for men discharged from Melbourne Gaol. The 'Prison-Gate Brigade' was the first permanent social service of its kind anywhere in the world. The Salvo's founder General William Booth's response to social welfare can probably best be summed up in this quote:

> *While women weep, as they do now, I'll fight; while children go hungry, as they do now, I'll fight; while men go to prison, in and out, in and out, as they do now, I'll fight; while there is a drunkard left, while there is a poor lost girl upon the streets, while there remains one dark soul without the light of God, I'll fight, I'll fight to the very end!*

During the Great Depression of the 1930s, Christian charity groups became the major source of relief for many Australians. The Christian vision in Australia from the earliest days was profoundly woven around health, education and social welfare. It is still the case. Organisations with a Christian base still dominate the delivery of welfare services throughout Australia.

It is not surprising that 23 of the 25 largest Australian charities, including World Vision, the Salvation Army, Compassion Australia, Australian Red Cross, Caritas and the St Vincent de Paul Society, have Christian foundations. These faith-based organisations have a major role in the welfare sector with the core value of achieving social justice for the most vulnerable. The Australian Charities and Not-for-profits Commission reported in 2015 that faith-based organisations are 'by far the largest single category of charities in Australia'.

Our faith-based organisations deliver a wide and diverse range of welfare needs, including emergency relief, provisions for housing and homelessness, health, mental health, education, community development, advocacy, research, income support and other social services. Australia's welfare system still relies heavily on charity – many of them Christian-based – rather than the state, to respond to the needs of marginalised people.

'The Beveridge Report', published in 1942, launched the welfare state and creation of a National Health Service with free health care in the United Kingdom. Liberal economist William Beveridge proposed widespread reforms to the system of social welfare to address what he identified as 'five giants on the road of post-war reconstruction – want, disease, ignorance, squalor and idleness'.

The idea of a welfare state did not take off in Australia. Then-prime minister Robert Menzies argued against everyone being dependent on the state. In a speech he said:

> I do not believe that we shall come out (of the war years) into the overlordship of an all-powerful state on whose benevolence we shall live, spineless and effortless – a state which will dole out bread and ideas with neatly regulated accuracy; where we shall all have our dividend without subscribing our capital; where the government, that almost deity, will nurse us and rear us and maintain us and pension us and bury us; where we shall all be civil servants, and all presumably, since we are equal, heads of departments.

The Commonwealth Government continued its wide support of faith-based welfare. This was a healthy realisation that Governments didn't have all the answers and that partnership with Christian charities was sensible and beneficial to all Australians.

Menzies, who described himself as a simple Presbyterian, was heavily influenced by the Methodist faith and had a strong focus on the dignity of individuals. Under his government, Australian foreign aid rose to its highest level ever and Australia's refugee intake was the highest in the world on a per capita basis. That came from both Menzies' understanding of his own faith and his belief that we are blessed to be a blessing. He refused to be obsessed, as too many governments are today, with a cost/benefit analysis.

After Menzies, governments increasingly became responsible for providing social services. Commonwealth unemployment and sickness benefits were introduced to provide income support to people who were out of work and the Commonwealth Employment Service was also established to provide assistance to unemployed people in seeking employment. But the work and influence of the charitable sector has continued.

More recently, faith-based organisations have had to compete for government funding with a rising number of secular counterparts. Reliance on government funding has led to some downplaying their Christian essence and identity. But evangelist and Nobel Peace Prize winner John Mott puts the Christian ethos quite simply: 'Evangelism without social work is deficient; social work without evangelism is impotent'.

Christian charitable activities make a vital contribution to the economic, social and political sectors of our nation. One of the most crucial kinds of Christian intervention is in advocacy. Christian charities must continue delivering services and also advocate for governments to establish fairer systems. Our advocacy as Christians to question the real causes of poverty and injustice is vital. Proverbs 31 says: 'Speak up for those who cannot speak for themselves, for the rights of all who are destitute. Speak up and judge fairly; defend the rights of the poor and needy'.

A recent Administrative Appeals Tribunal ruling that found benevolent institutions are allowed to advocate for political change is a welcome change. It is likely to embolden charities to directly pursue political change without fear. Christian charities always understood they are actually about two things: practical love, and change. Advocacy is fundamental to change. Australian churches play leading roles in this.

After the events in Kabul surrounding the withdrawal of US and other allied troops in August 2021, Micah, a Christian organisation I work with, helped to coordinate the Christians United for Afghanistan campaign, which calls on the Federal Government to provide a special intake of an additional 20,000 Afghan refugees. Many secularists view our churches as anti-Muslim. But this campaign has unified major church denominations and organisations, including Sydney Anglicans, the Uniting Church in Australia, Baptists, Catholics, Pentecostals as well as the Australian Christian Lobby and Common Grace in the fight for the wellbeing of even non-Christian refugees. This historic coalition is a significant and welcome sign of Christian unity.

In my Melbourne suburb of Frankston, churches have been providing care for 31,000 residents each year with a social value estimated to be $4.5 million. This has been shown by an intensive survey undertaken in 2021 by an organisation called NAYBA, which does Impact Audits to measure social impact value of the Church in a given community.

The Church must continue to find its mission in the midst of marginalised communities. We do this by servant leadership. Jesus beautifully defined this. He said: 'Whoever wants to become great among you must be your servant, and whoever wants to be first must be your slave—just as the Son of Man did not come to be served, but to serve, and to give his life as a ransom for many'.

In the age of celebrity and individualism as sacrosanct, it seems to be an odd way to operate. Yet service to others is vital in the Christian worldview which asks the relevant questions – why am I here? What's wrong with the world, and how do we fix it? Love is the work of Christ – both in us and through us to the world.

Every relationship in the universe between God and his creation and between humans is driven by four dynamics – justice, mercy, love and faith. All four are interwoven and one cannot be emphasised to the exclusion of the others.

A 2020 McCrindle report on the future of the church in Australia states that many Christian leaders believe Australians have become disillusioned with the church as an institution. According to the report, this is partly due to church culture becoming detached from the everyday Australian experience, and partly because of a break in trust due to poor leadership examples from the church. The report states church and clerical abuse is the number one behaviour blocker stopping non-Christians from exploring Christianity.

Imagine what would happen if more Australians really believed we Christians loved and cared for them? Surely there would be fewer empty seats in our churches.

Service and community are at the heart of the way through. Our theology and our belief grounds us – the culture around us challenges us – but it is in service that we find the space in which to play out God's purpose and God's plan. That's what Christian faith is about – it remembers those the powerful may forget.

The Covid-19 pandemic has offered society an opportunity to recognise how broken we have become and focuses on the importance of health and welfare and the need to reset for the future. It has indeed shown the power of local community to support the vulnerable and isolated. Examples of neighbourly care have been manifold.

I write as an inhabitant of Melbourne, the most locked-down city in the world. So I know from experience what communities, and more specifically many local churches, have been doing to sustain both their members and the wider community. All of us are biologically connected by an invisible virus and all of us are vulnerable if we do not act together.

Growth means change and change involves the risk of stepping from the known to the unknown. If we want to live meaningfully and well we must help enrich the lives of others, because the value of a life is measured by the lives it touches. As Christ taught, the welfare of each of us is bound up with the welfare of others.

Rev Tim Costello AO is a Baptist Minister. He has been involved as a leader in areas of Social Justice and Christian Ethics for many years. He was CEO of World Vision Australia 2004-16. Currently he is Exec Director of Micah Australia and Senior Fellow for The Centre for Public Christianity.

THE CHRISTIAN CITIZEN

MARTYN ILES

The concept of citizenship

The deepest political and historical thinkers have always known the long-term health and survival of a society ultimately depends, not on a good ruler or even a good constitution, but on the virtue of its citizens.

When Republican Rome collapsed into rule by unjust emperors, the great historian Livy was adamant concerning the ultimate cause – it was, he believed, loss of moral rigour and civic spirit among the people years before – or, what Livy referred to as 'our moral decline'. He wrote, 'Of late years, wealth has made us greedy and self-indulgence has brought us, through every form of sensual excess, to be, if I may so put it, in love with death both individual and collective'. More recently in history Thomas Jefferson, author of the 'Declaration of Independence' (1776), said in his *Notes on the State of Virginia* (1784), 'It is the manners and spirit of a people which preserve a republic in vigour. A degeneracy in these is a canker which soon eats to the heart of its laws and constitution'. John Stuart Mill in his *Representative Government* (1861) reaffirmed the ancient wisdom when he said, 'the first element of good government' is 'the virtue and diligence of the human beings composing the community'.

All of this is to agree with Scripture. The Biblical writer of Proverbs (14:34) said, 'Righteousness exalts a nation, but sin is a disgrace to any people'. Certainly, the Old Testament provides ample illustrations of nations suffering misery and trial because of the moral and religious decline of their people. Take the words of the Prophet Isaiah as but one example (30:1, 12-13), 'Woe to the obstinate children, declares the Lord, to those that carry out plans that are not mine… Because you have rejected the message, relied on oppression, and depended on deceit, this sin will become for you like a high wall, cracked and bulging, that collapses suddenly, in an instant'.

But these words recorded by Isaiah were not God's last word to a nation that has turned its back on His 'message' and 'Spirit'. More on that later.

Citizenship comes from the Latin for city – civitas – and refers to those virtues and rights that attach to members of the city that are necessary to maintain the health of the whole. Of course, nowadays, we don't talk about cities as the political unit. We talk about states and countries. So, by citizenship, I am not simply talking about legal status – my citizenship as an Australian – but first and foremost, I am talking about a set of virtues that ensure the preservation of the health of a country or nation state, when exercised by its citizens.

Citizenship has been understood this way since the Ancient Greeks, right up until the mid-twentieth century. It means that citizenship entails active outreach and involvement – it is duty-centric; not passive and receptive – rights-centric. To adapt a phrase from Sir Robert Menzies' 'The Forgotten People' speech (1942), the good citizen asks not how he can qualify society to advantage himself, but how he can qualify himself to advantage society.

When it comes to Christian citizens, the Bible is their foundation for living. Its teaching certainly supports these principles and enriches them with the requisite virtues. For example, there can be no arguing that the Biblical, Christian notion of citizenship is duty-centric, because Christian citizenship is a most important way of obeying Christ's command to love God and neighbour (Mark 12:31) – the two supreme duties in the

Christian's life. At the core of the duty to love God is the duty to keep His commandments (John 14:15), which is the same as saying a duty to be thoroughly virtuous in all things; a virtue that springs up from within a person, to be seen and encountered by those around them. The Christian's compulsion to serve God privately and publicly is a powerful source of the virtues necessary to preserve the health of a society. Meanwhile, the subsidiary duty to love our neighbours means a duty to demonstrate the same virtues to them, for their good. It can be expressed through aiding those in need, giving to charities, entering politics to advance good laws, and a host of other things which contribute to society's health and flourishing. All of this is Christian citizenship, because it is grounded in love of neighbour, grounded in obedience to Christ (1 John 4:7-12).

History testifies to the salutary influence of Christian citizenship on society. Perhaps the most spectacular modern example is the life-long activism of William Wilberforce (1759–1833) who worked towards the abolition of the slave trade (1807) and then towards the abolition of slavery within the British Empire (1833). Christian civic activism was also powerful in America in terms of critiquing slavery and, later, segregation, particularly in the anti-segregation Christian activism of the 1950s and 1960s. American political scientist Robert Woodbury's pioneering research into evangelical Protestant missionaries also shows that Christians in the European colonies in Africa, Latin America, Oceania, and Asia 'were a crucial catalyst initiating the development and spread of religious liberty, mass education, mass printing, newspapers, voluntary organisations, and colonial reforms, thereby creating the conditions that made stable democracy more likely'.

In Australia, Evangelical Protestants and Catholics were immensely influential in establishing civil society institutions such as charities, schools, banks, and newspapers. The work of historians such as Stuart Piggin and Robert Linder, who recorded the massive impact of evangelical

Christianity in Australia, shows that Christian citizenship was probably the most formative influence shaping Australia up until at least the mid-twentieth century, and one of the most influential until today.

Civil society and the Leviathan

The seminal research of American sociologist Robert Putnam established, in Putnam's words, that 'religious affiliation [was] by far the most common associational membership among Americans'. His work, summarised in his now-classic book *Bowling Alone: The Collapse and Revival of American Community* (2000), discussed the importance of what sociologists and political scientists call social capital. Social capital refers to the virtues, practices, and non-governmental institutions and intermediary organisations that create a flourishing society and thereby obviate the need for state intervention in the lives of communities.

Perhaps the most important aspect of social capital is a strong civil society or the presence of mediating institutions. Civil society or mediating institutions are those non-state-governmental institutions that secure for individuals the things they need to live flourishing lives: emotional stability, cheer, creative outlet, economic opportunity, relationships, economic and other forms of aid. Quintessential mediating institutions of civil society include the family, churches, small businesses, charities, and voluntary organisations.

Once these civil society institutions break down social problems, including crime, poverty, and family breakdown emerge and necessitate government intervention in an attempt to fix them. Unfortunately, too often what happens is 'solutions' are not tailored to local conditions and thus are ineffective, and bureaucracies become big, inefficient and expensive and thus divert funds from the problems themselves to the costs of maintaining the very bureaucracies whose job it is to fix them.

There are at least two reasons why we want strong civil society institutions. First, local, grassroots institutions like churches and charities understand the needs of local communities better than bureaucrats in far-away national/state capitals and are thus more likely to deliver services that meet the needs of local communities. This is often called the principle of subsidiarity, which has a long tradition in both Catholic and Protestant social thought. Subsidiarity – from the Latin word for 'help'– teaches that governments are best off using/outsourcing many services to local organisations rather than trying to directly provide all peoples/ communities' needs themselves.

The principle of subsidiarity does not necessarily teach that governments should not be involved in addressing social problems such as homelessness, family breakdown, domestic violence, delinquency, teenage pregnancy, or poverty, but that the first question governments should ask is not 'How can the government fix this?' but 'Are there any local people/ institutions/organisations already committed to solving these problems and if so how can the government help them?'.

Second, the more we depend on governments to provide the things we need to live flourishing lives, the more powerful governments are. If we depend on the government for our incomes, goods, services, and creative and relational outlets – clubs, etc – then the government can place conditions on these things and switch off our access to them if we fail to meet these conditions.

The breakdown of civil society and the resultant decline in social capital over the past sixty years has been disastrous not just for social health but also in terms of providing an opportunity for government to become an insatiable Leviathan.

In his book *Why Liberalism Failed*, Patrick Deneen outlined the logic of the relationship between moral, familial, and civil society break down and the ever-growing state in many Western societies. Deneen points out that with the replacement of Christian morality, with its emphasis on self-restraint and considering others' needs before one's own (Philippians 2:3), and the decline of church attendance, where such values are learned, social problems become exacerbated and necessitate increased government intervention in our lives. The full story is complex and cannot merely be reduced to the decline of Christianity, but a post-Christian morality of individualistic happiness must surely dim the sense of obligation that individuals have towards their spouses, families, and wider communities when living up to our obligations becomes a strain, as it invariably does.

Power always seeks to expand, not contract, and the same is true of the most powerful institution in modern society: the state. As substance abuse, crime, mental health and delinquency become worse in Western societies, and the civil institutions best able to address these problems and their underlying causes continue to erode, the only solution left becomes the state. As a result, government bureaucracies become packed with ideological 'problem solvers' who believe increased state intervention beginning with family life, speech, religious institutions and education is the solution.

Thus, if Christianity is good for mental and physical health, not to mention the happiness of spouses and the strength of families, then Christianity is good not only for keeping societies happy but also for ensuring the wicked social problems that provide an opportunity for the state to expand are kept at bay. Christianity is good for freedom, but only if we understand this freedom to be freedom from state interference in our affairs, not freedom from duties and obligations. As our concept of liberty became divorced from Christian morality, liberty became license, and license compromises our liberty, as explained above.

The following studies and statistics show the salutary effect of religion, particularly Christianity, on social capital. Such research is also important as a way of understanding one long-term strategy to counter the

Western trend of social and familial breakdown and the state expanding increasingly into our communities and families: a revival of Christianity. Christianity is good for society, not because Christians say so, but because the best statistical studies so testify.

Social benefits of faithful citizenship

A 2019 Pew Research Center report showed that in the US regular participation in a religious community was clearly linked with higher levels of civic activity (both voting in elections and being active in community groups/voluntary organisations). In brief, 58% of actively religious adults were also active in at least one other (nonreligious) kind of voluntary organisation, including charity groups, sports clubs or labour unions; as opposed to only about half of all inactively religious adults (51%) and fewer than half of the unaffiliated (39%).

The study also looked at other countries and similarly found that actively religious citizens are also more likely to be active in non-religious, civic-voluntary organisations.

Interestingly, the same study indicated that on balance, actively religious people are more likely to vote. In the US, a higher percentage of actively religious adults (69%) say they always vote in national elections than do inactives (59%) or the unaffiliated (48%). As Australia has compulsory voting no such studies have been carried out.

Charities

A 2015 Curtin University report stated that faith-based charities make an 'enormous and arguably under-recognised contribution to Australia's social infrastructure and social well-being'. Furthermore, such charities are 'by far the largest single category of charity in Australia'. Also, volunteers for religious charities represent 25% of all such volunteers in Australia. This corresponds with the data published by Koenig (see below), who found that of the twenty best studies into the relationship between religious/spiritual citizens (R/S), 75% of them reported a positive relationship.

Research from Dunham+Company (conducted by McCrindle, which surveyed over 1000 Australians) in 2016 showed 'churchgoers are three times more likely to give over $1000 annually to charity and give a far higher percentage of their income than the average Australian'.

The report concluded that:

- 15% of regular attenders give over $1,000 annually compared to only 5% of other Australians.
- Churchgoers 'give more often, with 79% giving in the last month compared with only 52% of irregular or non-attenders'.
- The 'average churchgoer' gave 0.7% of their income, as opposed to the average Australian taxpayer who gave 0.32% of their taxable income in tax-deductible donations in 2012-2013.
- Churchgoers are 'also the most responsive to requests for charitable gifts both online and through the mail'.

From a 2017 national survey of over 7,000 Australians a Deloitte Access Economics report showed that 'religious people are more likely to be donors and volunteers than non-religious people'. More specifically, religiosity is associated with 194,320 additional volunteers in Australia each year who collectively contribute 30.5 million hours in volunteering time. Furthermore, conversion to religion, according to the Deleoitte study, has a profound impact on volunteering. An average person who does not attend religious services and did not as a child has a 38% likelihood of being a volunteer. Comparatively, the average person who transitions from not attending as a child to attending as an adult has a 63% likelihood of being a volunteer. That is, people who transition from being non-religious to religious have a 25% higher likelihood of being volunteers.

Similar trends are evident elsewhere. A 2017 Giving USA report showed that 62% of religious households give to charity, compared with 46% of households with no religious affiliation. On average, religiously affiliated households donate $1,590 (US) to charity annually, while households with no religious affiliation contribute $695 (US). Also in the US the Philanthropy Roundtable found in 2019 that seven out of ten weekly church attenders said they consider 'work to help the needy' an 'essential part' of their faith. Furthermore, among Americans who attend services weekly and pray daily, 45% did volunteer work in the previous week, compared to 27% of other Americans.

Health and Happiness

The literature showing the social benefits of faithful citizens is vast and growing. Faithful citizenship is associated with the following trends and practices that promote social capital and ameliorate social maladies:

- volunteering and related positive character traits;
- positive mental health outcomes and fewer mental health conditions;
- lower levels of delinquency/crime and substance abuse;
- less marital instability;
- better physical health outcomes and personal health decisions; and
- reduced mortality overall.

Thus, research indicates that faithful citizens benefit society in two important ways:

1. directly to ameliorate social maladies;
2. indirectly by more likely avoiding behaviour linked to personal and social dysfunction.

Harold G. Koenig in his 2012 meta-analysis ('Religion, Spirituality, and Health: The Research and Clinical Implications', ISRN Psychiatry) of c.3300 articles investigating religious/spiritual (R/S) people and health concluded 'A large volume of research shows that people who are more R/S have better mental health and adapt more quickly to health problems compared to those who are less R/S'.

A 2016 study from the Harvard T.H. Chan School of Public Health published in the *American Journal of Epidemiology* found that people who attended weekly religious services or practiced daily prayer or meditation in their youth reported greater life satisfaction and positivity in their 20s. Also, such people were less likely to have depression, smoke, use illegal drugs, or have a sexually transmitted disease.

More recently, the 2019 Pew Research Center study 'Religion's Relationship to Happiness, Civic Engagement and Health Around the World', which relied heavily on data from mostly Christian-majority nations, found that actively religious people are: more likely to vote; more likely to engage in other types of groups; tend to be happier than others; and are most likely to abstain from frequent drinking and smoking.

In 2019 researchers W. Bradford Wilcox, Laurie DeRose, and Jason S. Carroll published 'The Ties that Bind: Is Faith a Global Force for Good or Ill in the Family?'. The research was commissioned by the Institute for Family Studies and Wheatley Institution. This major meta-analysis showed highly religious couples are much more likely to get married, and that when it comes to relationship quality in heterosexual relationships, highly religious couples enjoy higher-quality relationships and more sexual satisfaction, compared to less/mixed religious couples and secular couples. This means that higher religious couples are more likely to get married, stay together, and therefore raise socially well-adjusted children.

Christianity and harm
The reality is, in addition to its other benefits, Christianity is a positive social good and is important in order to counter the continued and

ongoing attacks on Christianity. These attacks centre on the accusation that Christianity is harmful. In turn, the supposed 'harm' caused by Christianity will underpin justifications to limit religious liberty. However, far from being harmful, the above research and statistics show that Christianity is beneficial for health, families, and society, and thus those who genuinely wish to minimise social harm should encourage Christianity, not discourage or punish it.

The contention that Christianity is harmful is unlike attacks on Christianity that emerged out of the radical Enlightenment of the eighteenth century – particularly in France – which attacked Christianity for being unscientific or unenlightened. Our age is aptly described as a therapeutic age, an age in which physical and mental health are judged by many to be the key to the good life. As Carl Trueman says in his brilliant *Rise and Triumph of the Modern Self* (2020), we have witnessed 'the slow and steady transformation of all areas of public life by the therapeutic'. Culturally, Western civilisation has moved from Jesus' understanding of happiness or blessedness as living in humble, loving, hope and expectation of God's Kingdom fully revealed in Christ's return and reign (Matt 5:1-13, 4-48; 6:9-13), to happiness defined in terms of pleasure, self-esteem, and positive feelings.

To quote Salvatore Babones' book *The New Authoritarianism* (2018), we have gone from 'the right to pursue happiness to the right to be happy'. But if happiness is a right, then it becomes very easy to see those who do not make us happy, or who make us unhappy because of their words or their beliefs, as violating others' right to be happy. At this point it becomes plausible to demand that the state intervene and stop these purveyors of anti-happiness by outlawing speech and religious practices. As Trueman says, 'Once harm and oppression are regarded as being primarily psychological categories, freedom of speech then becomes part of the problem, not the solution, because words become potential weapons'.

Increasingly, any comment or argument seen as offensive is immediately condemned as 'hate speech'.

Rod Dreher picks up much of this thread in his *Live Not By Lives: A Manual for Christian Dissidents*. Against many who think that predictions of a rising totalitarianism in the West are alarmist throwbacks to the Cold War, Dreher makes some qualifications. For Dreher, the coming totalitarianism won't be jackboots and goosesteps. On the contrary, 'This totalitarianism is therapeutic'. It will be a soft totalitarianism, says Dreher, one in which our lives will be increasingly governed and controlled by governments and corporations via unprecedented technology for the sake of our health and wellbeing.

The West's response to Covid should make it impossible for anyone to call Dreher, Trueman, or those before them alarmist.

In our emerging therapeutic society, some things will be deemed healthy and worthy of promotion – like self-expression, pleasure, sexual experimentation – and others will be deemed unhealthy, harmful, and oppressive – like biblical teachings on sexuality, gender, the nuclear family, life, and other flashpoint social issues.

Biblical Christianity is still being tolerated for the most part, but once its status as 'harmful' becomes embedded in public policy, medical bureaucracies, and new human rights laws, then biblical moral teachings, especially around matters like gender and sexuality, will increasingly be outlawed in education, speech, and practice. The Victorian 'Change or Suppression (Conversion) Practices Prohibition Bill 2020' embodies everything about our therapeutic age discussed by Trueman and others. This bill treats biblical views of sexuality, sin, and gender as harmful and seeks to criminalise practices that express them – even practices as benign as prayers or speech. It is a portent of things to come.

Conclusion

As long as civic virtue is essential for the health of society, and for maintaining the proper bounds of the state, Christian citizenship is important. The studies and statistics I have cited show that Christian conviction and church attendance are good for the wellbeing of individuals, of families, and therefore of society. Furthermore, Christians are more likely to be involved, not just in church, but in their wider communities through non-religious organisations and voting in elections. Christianity is the best social capital a democratic nation can have.

Indeed, in terms of our quantitative understanding of the character traits that make for good citizenship, the single most valuable character trait is to be a disciple of Jesus Christ. Yes, I mean to say that the best thing for society is for more people to repent and believe the gospel, and go on following Jesus.

Practically, this means – at the very least – that governments should not inhibit the free expression of religion, or the establishment of institutions that spread religion – Christianity in particular. In countries with a Christian heritage, statespersons should not feel inhibited from commending churchgoing, scripture teaching, and Christian conviction, for in doing so they encourage something that is statistically proven to be good for the nation as a whole.

But Christianity is not merely beneficial. It is also true. This means that it will endure, and many followers of Jesus Christ will continue not only to believe, but to be infectious, as He commanded them to be. They will be strengthened in their resolve, finding fresh urgency and purpose, as they watch Western society continue to unchain itself from its roots. The West is spinning into a therapeutic vortex, seeking to substitute Christianity for climate alarmism, identity politics and now anti-Covid zeal. Meanwhile, families continue to disintegrate, loneliness gnaws away at more lives, individuals continue to fall into rising rates of depression and addiction and children are falling victim to distorted understandings of gender and sexuality. Such a society is craving for truth to set it free, and the Christian has good news to tell on that front.

Jesus said the following words in Matthew 5:14-16:

> *You are the light of the world. A town built on a hill cannot be hidden. Neither do people light a lamp and put it under a bowl. Instead they put it on its stand, and it gives light to everyone in the house. In the same way, let your light shine before others, that they may see your good deeds and glorify your Father in heaven.*

Disciples of Jesus Christ must be 'the light of the world' – that is, engage visibly in Christian citizenship, to serve God and neighbour and especially to create other disciples of Jesus Christ.

But we should be under no illusions that everyone will become a true Christian. Jesus Himself rejects such optimism. Still, we can be sure that all that is needed to help put individuals, families, communities, and whole societies on a better track is a strong core of followers of Christ who are committed to Christian citizenship. Perhaps Christian citizenship can, in the long run, testify to the enduring truth of the risen Lord Jesus, as it influences society in seemingly miraculous ways, ameliorating the most wicked problems, from domestic violence to indigenous disadvantage. It has done so in the past and it can do so again.

To return to the prophet Isaiah, God never left the Israelites without a means of redemption; a way to make things right again. 'In repentance and rest is your salvation, in quietness and trust is your strength...' The Israelites may have rejected God's plea for repentance in this instance, but the offer stands for all people who wish to abandon lives of immorality, selfishness, addiction and rebellion against the God who made and sustains them. God's offer of salvation and reconciliation is available, not first to nations, but to individuals – every person who turns from their sin and lives as a subject or follower of the Lord Jesus Christ (John 3:16; Rom 1:13; 1 John 3:23-24; 5:3).

If you are a true follower of Jesus Christ then you know that you must not merely be a citizen, but a Christian citizen. If you are not, now you know how you can be. And take heart in the words of Jesus, 'Then you will know the truth, and the truth will set you free' (John 8:32).

Martyn Iles is a lawyer, commentator, and the Managing Director of the Australian Christian Lobby (ACL), one of Australia's largest political movements. ACL brings truth into the public squares through people-powered campaigns, parliamentary lobbying, and mainstream and alternative media.

CHRISTIANITY UNDER ATTACK

WANDA SKOWRONSKA

Christianity is increasingly under attack in today's world. These attacks take many forms including direct physical attacks; and indirect attacks through political and psychological means which undermine the beliefs of Christians living in societies increasingly permeated by a strident secularism intolerant of the Judeo-Christian worldview.

The 2021 'Religious Freedom in the World Report' commissioned by Aid to the Church in Need, found direct attacks on religious freedom occur in one third of the world's countries (62 out of 196), especially in populous nations such as China, India, and Pakistan. It found that the level of oppression 'has increased in nearly all listed as the survey's worst offenders'.[26] Moreover, the consistent finding is that the most intensely persecuted believers in the world today are Christians, and the most attacked belief system is Christianity.

Other findings repeat this sad reality, among them, the regular reports of the United Nations (UN) Special Rapporteur on 'Freedom of Religion or Belief'; the Pew Research Centre; and the Independent Review completed by the Anglican Bishop of Truro in the Province of Canterbury, the Reverend Philip Mounstephen. The Bishop concluded in 2019 that Christians are the most widely targeted religious community in the world. They constitute 80% of those attacked and:

26 https://acnuk.org/our-campaigns/religious-freedom-in-the-world-report-2021/

> *acts of violence... against Christians are becoming more*
> *widespread and severe... In parts of the Middle East and Africa,*
> *the vast scale of the violence and its perpetrators' declared intent to*
> *eradicate the Christian community, has led to several Parliamentary*
> *declarations in recent years that the faith group has suffered genocides*
> *according to the definition adopted by the UN.*[27]

The physical attacks on Christianity include kidnapping, threats of violence, general harassment, legal discrimination, media and cyberspace incitement to hatred, detention, and imprisonment. The consequences are internal dislocation, exodus, and martyrdom. Many lament the fate of Christianity in the Middle East where its roots go back the furthest to the time of Christ and the New Testament. In Syria, Iraq and other parts of the Middle East, Christianity is at risk of disappearing altogether. A century ago, Christians constituted 20% of the Middle East population; today that figure is less than 4%. Plurality, which was key to security and stability in the region for centuries, is waning. Egypt's Coptic Christians, mostly Orthodox, with up to 1 million Evangelical Christians and 250,000 Catholics, are increasingly under attack, risking their lives by going to church. On Palm Sunday in 2017, Islamic State suicide bombers targeted two Coptic churches, killing at least 44 people and injuring dozens more.

Former British Chief Rabbi Lord Jonathan Sacks told the House of Lords: 'The persecution of Christians throughout much of the Middle East, sub-Saharan Africa and Asia, [and] elsewhere is one of the crimes against humanity of our time and I'm appalled at the lack of protest it has evoked'.[28] Journalist John Allen stated several years ago that, 'In effect, the world is witnessing the rise of an entire new generation of Christian martyrs. The carnage is occurring on such a vast scale that it represents not only the most dramatic Christian story of our time, but arguably the

27 https://christianpersecutionreview.org.uk/report/
28 Ibid.

premier human rights challenge of this era as well' (*Spectator*, 5 October 2013). With example after example, Allen observes that this attack is not limited to a 'clash of civilisations' between Christianity and Islam. In *The Global War on Christians: Dispatches from the Front Lines of Anti-Christian Persecution* (2016), he states that Christians face a bewildering variety of threats everywhere with no single enemy and no single strategy to counter them. Both Allen and Rabbi Sacks have noted this attack on Christians is one of the most underreported stories of our times; often because local reporters are under threat of death for reporting it or because the Western media who could report it do not do so. While Angela Merkel has made passing reference to the fact that Christianity is the 'world's most persecuted religion', as do some world leaders, there is a certain Western blindness, glossing over one of the greatest eras of persecution and martyrdom in recent history.

Why is this so? There are myriad answers to this question. Mainly in the second form of attack mentioned above – the ongoing political/psychological undermining of Christianity by the Western media and educational institutions. Some point to post-colonial attitudes, the Crusades, the post-modern rejection of coherent belief systems, cultural Marxism, the paedophilia scandals, and moral relativism in the West. Some go back to the French Revolution's attempt to dethrone religion. As Roger Scruton remarks in *The West and the Rest* (2007), it is impossible to understand the French Revolution without seeing it as a religious phenomenon, seeking to replace religion with 'religiously' pursued earthly empires.

And the religion to be exterminated was undeniably Christianity; ignoring the West's Christian roots and the fact that much of Western civilisation's art, music and literature can only be understood in its Christian context and reference to transcendental realities. This anti-Christian zeal burgeoned in the nineteenth century with Marx, Nietzsche, in various forms of utopian world building and overweening faith in human progress. Now, however, more emphasis is given to an event almost hidden at the time, yet of pivotal importance in history – the establishment of the Frankfurt School in Germany in 1923. The past century's attack on Christianity cannot be properly accounted for without understanding the profound impact of the Frankfurt School; especially on the West's universities.

After the failed Communist attempts to conquer Poland (1918–20), Munich (1918–19), and Hungary (1920), Lenin was so incensed there was much shoe-throwing rage within the walls of the Kremlin. How was he to bring down Western civilisation if its armies and workers militarily opposed the irrefutable logic of Soviet progress? The idea of a non-military way of attacking the West was conceived at Moscow's Marx-Engels Institute in 1920–1922; a form of social and political control, a constant insertion of anti-Western ideas into major institutions, including the media, education and even religious organisations.

Lenin established the Frankfurt Institute, aided by Félix José *Weil*, a German-Argentinian Marxist who had inherited wealth and nothing better to do with it than to spread Marxist ideology. In a post-industrial era, the Institute tapped into a new desire to analyse and reconstruct Western societies, interweaving Marxist ideas with the prevailing sense of dislocation, angst, and unstoppable change. It fuelled an obsession to meld state, culture, and religion into new political entities. For example, supposed care for working people became a central principle of a Communist state, replacing religious beliefs with Marxist/Leninist ideology, which ushered in total control of social and cultural life.

One of the Institute's media organisers, Communist Wilhelm 'Willi' Münzenberg, used his charms to infiltrate Western media, influencing naïve Western journalists, writers, and Hollywood producers, seen as 'Innocents' (later called 'useful idiots'), to support the Soviet view. Many in the West were seduced, as revealed by Ion Mihai Pacepa, the highest-ranking defector from the Soviet Union, in his book *Red Horizons: Chronicles of a Communist Spy Chief* (1987) and by Vladimir Bukovsky in *Judgement in Moscow; Soviet Crimes and Western Complicity* (2019).

One of the most useful idiots, writes journalist Greg Sheridan (*The Australian*, 8 November 2019), was Australia's historian Manning Clark who, in *Meeting Soviet Man* (1960), described Lenin as 'Christ-like' and saw Communist victories in Eastern Europe, China and Vietnam in visionary terms as indicators of human progress. This would have been news to the more than 60 million killed by the Communist regime and further millions suffering in the gulags.

These new western social 'experts' of the 1920s onwards tapped into post-war psychological angst. Westerners, with an irresistible sense of grievance were sitting ducks. One excellent account of such Marxist influence in politics is related in Stanton Evans' and Herbert Romerstein's *Stalin's Secret Agents: the Subversion of Roosevelt's Government*. A more personal account is *Witness* (1952), by Whittaker Chambers, American journalist, Communist Party member and Soviet agent, who learnt skills in deception from the 1930s onwards, working feverishly to undermine his own society and its cultural base. Strange to say, in the end Chambers left it all and turned to God.

The Frankfurt Institute academics – Theodore Adorno, Herbert Marcuse, William Reich among many others, while never mentioning Communism, wooed academia, continually attacking Christianity out of a professed need to be 'liberated' from older views of culture and history. When they left Frankfurt, before and after the Second World War, the new 'experts' were welcomed at other universities, particularly Columbia in New York, where generations of teachers and academics were influenced by their anti-Western, anti-Christian dogma. Western society was certainly not psychologically immunised against this all-out attack, nor from the anti-religious views of Sigmund Freud. In the 1970s, I recall the name 'Marcuse' being mentioned at Sydney University, amidst growing denigration of any Christian views.

Even though '[t]he great world religions are, as it were, great rivers of sacred tradition which flow down through the ages and through changing historical landscapes'; and even though art, science, universities, and the understanding of the dignity of the human person arose from Christendom (Christopher Dawson, *Religion, and the Rise of Western Culture*, 1955), there was now a continual, planned onslaught on Christianity. As the Italian Marxist Antonio Gramsci proposed, there would be a 'long march through the institutions', presenting a godless world rid of its Western culture, as if this were its natural evolution. Phillip Salzman stated:

> *The one place that Marxism has succeeded is in conquering academia in Europe and North America. Marxism-Leninism is now the dominant model of history and society being taught in Western universities and colleges. Faculties of social science and humanities disguise their Marxism under the label 'postcolonialism,' anti-neoliberalism, and the quest for equality and 'social justice.' And while our educational institutions laud 'diversity' in gender, race, sexual preference, religion, national origin, etc., diversity in opinion, theory, and political view is nowhere to be seen. So, our students hear only the Marxist view.*

'Marxism Failed in the World but Conquered Western Academia' History, language, education, and psychology departments from the 1960s onwards were increasingly permeated with a sense that Western civilisation was, above all, oppressive. A special form of social critique arose – Critical Theory – a critique of a supposedly failing capitalist society (ironically at a time when wages were rising for workers!). Critical Theory did not aim specifically at economic destruction, but attacked the cultural superstructure, the beliefs held by the society. And what beliefs specifically? The Christian worldview of course. Many would not have picked up the post-modern narrative at that time – who really knew where things were going in the 1960s and '70s?

The view that the West is irredeemably bad because it is racist, sexist, misogynistic, homophobic, xenophobic, unfair, and transphobic hit universities big-time from 1980s onwards. The past undeniable evils of some racists, colonialists, and paedophiles, now applied to all Western civilisation. Critical race theory and post-colonial theory have so affected humanities courses that students apologise for their Western, Christian backgrounds, as indicators of being oppressors.

In his widely read *Eros and Civilisation* (1956) Herbert Marcuse depicted Western culture as not only politically, but also personally oppressive, saying that (Western) culture constrains a person's inherent biological and instinctual structure (again, when gulags held millions in Marxist paradise!).

As Western intellectuals become more anti-Western and woke, an implacable hatred of its spiritual heritage was assumed. The current statue destroying tendencies cannot be compared to the iconoclasm of the past, which had at least some view of religion at its base. It is more a cancellation of historic memory – zero memory, zero culture. Such destruction of past memory was essential to the Stalinist worldview, with its elevation of worker heroes and history itself. Orwell's *Nineteen Eighty-Four* portrays a compliant bureaucrat, Winston Smith, who works in the Records Department of the Ministry of Truth, rewriting historical documents to match the continually changing current party line, denigrating the past. Ironically, wokesters may revere the doctors that treat them, yet despise the culture that produced them.

Polish philosopher and EU member Ryszard Legutko noted in *Totalitarian Demons in Democracy* (2016) that although Communism's economic systems had failed, Marxism's ideas of discontent with Christendom and traditional institutions, were now echoed in Western 'neo-Marxism' or 'cultural Marxism'. The social cohesion of millennia was deconstructed on every front through what Frank Furedi calls 'mental conditioning' and others 'social engineering'. After decades of defending Catholicism against Soviet onslaughts, Pope John Paul II encountered a West threatened by an academically inspired self-hatred.

This incursion of Marxism ironically fell in with the commercialisation of most universities, which renowned Australian scholar Pierre Ryckmans, who taught at the ANU and Sydney universities, termed 'bazaars hustling for students'. Similarly, the indefatigable defender of Christianity and reason, Paul Stenhouse MSC, observed in a 2003 Annals article:

> New recruits for a hypothetical 21st century post-modernist university dining-club at a university near you, would be bombarded with scepticism about the past and the present. 'The truth is unknowable and beyond the reach of us all,' they will be told. 'Historical research is impossible because history is "fiction".' 'The difference between historical "fact" and "falsehood" is ideological.' As we can't know anything about the past, it's better to ignore it; or to dismiss it as ideologically distorted by those who recorded it.

For those unfamiliar with the evolution of cancel culture, it is instructive to read the words of one of its victims, Peter Seewald, in a 2017 Catholic World Report article:

> During the student rebellions of 1968 I began to engage with politics. Christianity seemed something of a relic from the past then. I felt that its mixture of power and madness had to be overcome in order finally to build a genuinely progressive society. So, one day I withdrew myself from the Church. I felt liberated, and I fought for the ideas of Marx and Lenin.

Seewald did later return to his Catholic roots and ended up interviewing Pope Benedict XVI, who himself commented: 'Europe has developed a culture that in a way hitherto unknown to humanity excludes God from public consciousness… irrelevant for public life.' ('Europe in the Crisis of Cultures', *Communio*, 2005.)

The point to remember is that the West's tearing down of statues and concomitant hatred for Christianity did not happen suddenly. It was fuelled by the Frankfurt Institute's well planned anti-Western agenda, deriving from nineteenth century anti-Christian animus and the French Revolution. It was spurred on in the past century by a post-Auschwitz, post-war, post-everything trauma, ennui, and a desire for well-being. In 'Toward a New Totalitarianism' (1970) Augusto Del Noce astutely observed this Western slide into well-being, which like Marxism, sacrificed religious principles, also for materialist purposes. It did not represent a break with the fascist and totalitarian past but a transformation of Marxism into a new totalitarianism composed of 'scientism, eroticism, and the theology of secularisation'– in which citizens worldviews were narrowed to this worldly achievements and comfort. There was increasing indifference to the Western Christian past, and if there were any fervour, it was to deride it and rational discourse about any transcendent dimension.

A most sinister aspect of western destabilisation came with altered anthropologies. 'Person' became the most dangerous term of the twentieth century. Whereas for millennia, the Christian view of the person was of a union of body and soul, with inalienable dignity, now alternative views of the person were proposed in Nazism, Communism and in the Humanist Manifesto of 1933, dismissing any transcendent dimension. Governments and committees could decide whether people should live or die. While eastern Europe had its materialist Marx, the West had its Kool-Aid in Carl Rogers who dismissed the 'old' Judeo-Christian anthropology, saying that from a 'new revolution' would emerge 'a new kind of person, thrusting up through the dying, yellowing, putrefying leaves and stalks of our fading institutions'.

Carl Rogers on Personal Power (1977, 262). Rogers' *On Becoming a Person* (1961), used as a psychology textbook for decades, interpolated secular humanist empathy with anti-Christian animus, aiming at self-actualisation without any reference to any objective moral norms. The legacy of past wisdom was forgotten. And Christians flocked to Rogers's psychology courses, surreptitiously imbibing the pleasant but deadly assault on their Judeo-Christian legacy. This self-focus resonated with the emerging New Age focus on the divinised self, which not only turned away from past religions as sources of wisdom but also from reason itself. With no clear articulation of beliefs, the New Age presents a common anti-rational 'vision' of a future global transformation (some called it the Age of Aquarius) and it is not surprising that Rogers and Maslow eventually turned to this. The large New Age Centre established in California in 1962, called Esalen, attracted seekers of myriad spiritualities, all having in common a rejection of the Judeo-Christian past, many of them now leaders in western society. In *Catholics and the New Age* (1992), American Fr Mitch Pacwa describes his involvement in that era's heady spiritualities and how he, along with others, escaped it all.

The '60s Zeitgeist also affected theology, especially in the way Christ was depicted as a political revolutionary, a mythical figure, a hippie, a New Age seeker, or humanist social worker, anything but a transcendent Divine person. Such powerful images often work at greater depth than theories. Leonard Boff presented a politicised Christ and Deepak Chopra a New Age Christ (*The Third Jesus: The Christ We Cannot Ignore*, 2008). Most secularists were convinced that God was there to enhance their well-being. Few noticed the warning in Pope Paul VI's Populorum Progressio (1967, par 42):

*A narrow humanism closed in on itself and not open to the values
of the spirit and to God who is their source, could achieve apparent
success for man... But 'closed off from God [it] will end up being
directed against man. A humanism closed off from other realities
becomes inhuman'.*

This closing off from transcendent realities, the effect of anti-Christian,
cultural Marxist and woke assaults have altered the West profoundly.
American psychologist Paul Vitz, in *Faith of the Fatherless: the Psychology
of Atheism* (1999), reflected:

*Only as it starts to fade can we see how strange the modern
world has been... and nothing has been more typical of public life...
than the presumption of atheism. God has been banished from
public discourse... atheism is a recent and distinctively Western
phenomenon... no other culture has manifested such a widespread
public rejection of the divine.*

The rejection of the divine is notably evident in views of the family,
gender, and reality itself. There were continual calls for liberation from the
'oppressive, patriarchal' structure of the family by Margaret Sanger from
the 1920s onwards. As Joyce Milton writes in *The Road to Malpsychia:
Humanist Psychology and its Discontents* (2003), Margaret Mead and
Ruth Benedict announced that any other society was less repressive than
the West. To escape repression Alfred Kinsey founded the Institute for
Sex Research at Indiana University in 1947, now known as The Kinsey
Institute, researching sexual behaviours that would have had him arrested,
even today.

These continual assaults on the family targeted the recognition of
marriage as between a man and woman. On 9 December 2017, following
a referendum which many saw as entailing 'equality' and 'human rights'
issues, the right to marry in Australia was no longer determined by sex or
gender. As a psychologist I saw the infiltration of these views regarding

marriage, abortion and euthanasia presented as 'intellectual progress' into educational institutions and to question the need to foist such views on children was seen as primitive, repressive and anti-progress.

Perhaps the strongest recent attack on Christianity is the transgender assertion that you are not your biological gender but rather anyone out of a multitude of gender categories you want to be. As Kate Bornstein announced in *Gender Outlaw: Men Women and the Rest of* Us (1994), 'gender fluidity recognizes no borders or rules of gender'. This contradicted the fundamental beliefs of 2.3 billion Christians, not to mention billions of Jews, Hindus, Buddhists, Muslims, in fact, most of the world's citizens and views of non-religious figures, such as Camille Paglia, Martina Navratilova, Domenico Dolce, Stefano Gabbana, Germain Greer and JK Rowling who have publicly opposed transgenderism and argue a person's sex is biologically determined.

Again, transgenderism did not suddenly appear but was sparked over a century ago by German physician, Magnus Hirschfield (1868-1935) who categorised 64 possible genders. His views found support in New Zealander John Money, who completed his studies at Harvard and became professor of paediatrics and medical psychology at Johns Hopkins University. He furthered the notion of the social construction of gender from the 1950s onwards, writing *Man & Woman, Boy & Girl* (1972), used as a college level textbook.

One of John Money's first 'projects' at the Johns Hopkins gender change clinic involved the Canadian boy David Reimer, one of twin boys born in Manitoba in 1966. Reimer was born a male but due to damaged sex organs was 'reassigned' as a female from infancy onwards by Money. David was dressed in female clothes and attended regular sessions with Money. He was given the name Brenda and various operations were performed on him. Despite the frilly dresses, 'Brenda' did not feel he was a girl and was not accepted by female peers. The reassignment also involved his twin brother in various behaviours with his 'female' brother. From the age of 11 onward Reimer began to question his 'female' identity and then decided to live as a male from the age of 14, no longer attending sessions with Money. He suffered from severe depression and committed suicide in 2004. His twin brother committed suicide (earlier in 2002). No public comment on the 'failure' of this 'project' was issued by Money who dismissed any media criticism of it as 'right wing bias' and 'antifeminism'.

In 2013, the *Diagnostic and Statistical Manual of Mental Disorders* (DSM V edition) removed any negative reference to transgenderism as a Gender Identity Disorder, now using the more agreeable term 'Dysphoria'. Again, psychology had aided the attack on fundamental Christian beliefs as it had decades before, in pushing notions of liberation from any restraint. This represented a ground shift in Christendom, perpetrated by 'experts' and a politicisation of the helping professions and science. Interestingly, in 2014, Polish parish priests, emerging from 70 years of Communist attempts at socially constructing persons, read their parishioners a letter signed by all Catholic Bishops of the nation entitled 'The Dangers Stemming From Gender Ideology':

> *The gender ideology (movement) is the product of many decades of ideological and cultural changes that are deeply rooted in Marxism and neo-Marxism endorsed by some feminist movements and the sexual revolution. This ideology promotes principles that are totally contrary to reality and an integral understanding of human nature. It maintains that biological sex is not socially significant and that cultural sex, which humans can freely develop and determine irrespective of biological conditions, is most important...*

Some began to speak out against this denial of biological reality. Walt Heyer, who became Laura Jensen, described the profound damage done by his 'gender change'. He reverted to being male and wrote of it in *Paper Genders* (2011) to help others suffering in silence. Psychiatrists and paediatricians spoke out, including Professor Paul McHugh, Professor Michelle Cretella, Dr Richard Fitzgibbon, and Australian Professor John Whitehall, saying that the denial of biological reality was unscientific and wrong. Psychologist Jordan Peterson stopped a BBC interviewer in her tracks, suggesting she was 'totalitarian' in demanding he use transgender pronouns (a Canadian Law could fine citizens up to $250,000 for the novel crime of 'mis-gendering', not using new pronouns such as zie/hir, ey/em/ eir). Peterson's depiction of the BBC interviewer as totalitarian, reduced her to shocked babbling, witnessed by millions of viewers, a successful post-modern tactic against the woke brigade. Christians take note.

Strange to say, despite the secularising West, the world's population is not necessarily becoming less religious, for nearly 80% profess some religious belief. The most religious parts of the world have the fastest population growth because of high fertility rates and relatively young populations.[29] While there are around 2.3 billion Christians in the world today, and while they are demographically declining in the West, they still provide widespread welfare organisations in orphanages, refuges, missions, schools and shelters around the world.

Demographic growth is most dramatic, however, in the developing world, where Christians are mostly physically attacked. In its 2020 report, the Catholic Agenzia Fides noted that the number of major seminarians, diocesan and religious, had increased in Africa and Asia, with decreases in Europe and America. For example, Nigeria, with more than 200 million people, with its fast-growing rates of Christian believers (and martyrdom), now regularly exports priests and ministers to Western countries. Many demographers say the future of Christianity is African. United Nation projections say that the population of Africa will number 2.5 billion in 2050 and more than 4 billion in 2100. The

---

29 https://www.pewforum.org/2018/06/13/the-age-gap-in-religion-around-the-world/

Pew Centre predicts that in 2060, the top 6 countries with highest Christian populations will be Nigeria, Ghana, Kenya, Tanzania, Uganda, and Cameroon. Australian immigrants from South Korea and Vietnam have largely outnumbered locals in the Catholic Seminaries. And priests from India, Poland, and Africa figure increasingly among clergy in the Australian Christian churches.

In the jaded West spiritual seeking cannot be entirely exterminated, and courageous clergy and ordinary people challenge the Zeitgeist and occasionally Christian politicians get elected. While numbers of people with no religious affiliation grow, as Saint John Paul II stated, in 'Fides et Ratio' (1998), there are compelling questions which never go away, in every culture:

> Who am I? Where have I come from and where am I going? Why is there evil? What is there after this life? These are the questions which we find in the sacred writings of Israel as also in the Veda and the Avesat; we find them in the writings of Confucius and Lao-Tze and in the preaching of the Tirhankara and Buddha. They appear in the poetry of Homer and in the tragedies of Euripedes and Sophocles as they do in the philosophical writings of Plato and Aristotle. They are questions which have their common source in the quest for meaning which have always compelled the human heart. (John Paul II, Fides et Ratio, 1998, Par 1).

These questions will always persist. After the twin tower tragedy, television cameras recorded New Yorkers kneeling on the sidewalk, looking up, addressing Someone, as also happened around the recently burnt-out shell of Paris' Notre Dame. A formerly atheist Chinese man told me he watched the beatification of John Paul II on TV in 2011 (since no sport was on), and was converted by the ceremony, and is now a devout Catholic. An Indian lady of formerly Rastafarian belief told me she walked into a Christian church in Sydney one day and was so struck by 'something' that she also ended up on a journey to Christ. Another woman of 30 who had lost her faith on leaving school, happened to go to a monastery looking for 'inner peace' and found her way back to her Catholic faith. After experiencing hell on earth, Auschwitz survivor Viktor Frankl wrote *The Search for Meaning* (1946), one of the top ten selling books of the twentieth century, saying that spiritual seeking cannot be suppressed. There may yet be a return to God after the loss of God in the West. It may take unexpected forms, may not appear on census forms, but it cannot be destroyed. As Ecclesiastes puts it 'God has set eternity in the human heart' and the search remains when all else is lost.

Wanda Skowronska is a Catholic psychologist and author living and working in Sydney, Australia. She completed a PhD. at the John Paul II Institute in Melbourne in 2011 where she did sessional lecturing. She is author of several books including To Bonegilla from Somewhere *(2012),* Angels Incense and Revolution: Catholic Schooldays of the 1960s *(2019) and* Paul Stenhouse: a Life of Rare Wisdom, Compassion and Inspiration *(2021). She has written for several periodicals, including* Annals Australasia, Quadrant, Homiletic and Pastoral Review *and* The Catholic Weekly.

CHRISTIANITY'S SINS

PETER ROSENGREN

After more than a quarter of a century working on official Catholic newspapers in Australia, a period which has often included coverage of statements by bishops conferences and other official Catholic Church bodies and agencies, I can say that my all-time favourite bishops' conference last met somewhere around the year 909 AD. In that year, as recounted by the British historian Christopher Dawson in his 1948 Gifford lectures given at the University of St Andrews in Scotland, the bishops of the province of Rheims gathered at Trosle, a small village near present-day Soissons in France.

The Council of Trosle gathered under the presidency of Archbishop Herive of Rheims on the 26 June that year, early-summer. But the warmth of the season belied the state of the church and of the time. The tenth century has sometimes been called the Age of Iron regarding the Church and medieval society for its often-brutal nature and the deep-set corruption that had entered widely into the heart of the Catholic Church, then a key focus of learning and administrative authority – in the absence of anything else – in medieval society, and of civil power. While modern historians are constantly revising their readings of how 'dark' the Dark Ages really were (the period stretching from the final collapse of the *pax Romana* and the Roman Empire in the fifth century through until the Renaissance), the 15 proclamations signed by 12 prelates at the Council are a Jeremiad regarding the state of the Church and the state of their world in general. The bishops wrote:

Men devour one another like the fishes in the sea. In the case of the monasteries some have been destroyed by the heathen, others have been deprived of their property and reduced to nothing. In those that remain there is no longer any observance of the rule. They no longer have legitimate superiors, owing to the abuse of submitting to secular domination... We see in the monasteries, lay abbots with their wives and their children, their soldiers and their dogs.

But the prelates did not spare themselves either:

God's flock perishes through our charge. It has come about by our negligence, our ignorance and that of our brethren, that there is in the Church an innumerable multitude of both sexes and every condition who reach old age without instruction, so that they are ignorant even of the words of the Creed and the Lord's Prayer.

Despite the dire and pressing situation, this willingness to squarely face up to the true reasons for the corruption of the Church in their own time makes, I think, the bishops of Rheims an outstanding example to the rest of history, including to the Church in the twenty-first century. Yet Dawson, one of the most remarkable historians of western civilisation and culture, understood the significance of the bishops' confession perfectly: 'When the leaders of any society realise the gravity of the situation and admit their own responsibility like this,' he noted in his study of the intersection of European religion, culture and power, *Religion and the Rise of Civilisation*, 'the situation is never desperate'.

It's interesting, as an aside, to wonder how many bishops actually participated in the Council of Trosle. The 12 signatories may well have been far fewer than the numbers participating. One of the key problems of the age which they named was precisely what they described as an abuse by those (the abbots and bishops) who made up the Church's elite centres of their own authority and power: submission to secular domination. If there were more than the 12 signatories present, perhaps other clergy judged it too risky to office, personal position, wealth and power to bell the cat and thereby antagonise the local duke or lord.

But Dawson's assessment was correct: the willingness of the bishops of Trosle to name the problems confronting the Church and the absolute primacy of its mission of evangelisation can still be admired a millennium later. Clearly they had courage – no easy thing to possess in the midst of an age commonly characterised by corruption, brute force, nepotism and assassination as the usual means to resolve serious problems – and often problems that were not so serious. Not only was the state of the Church parlous in almost every regard, but much of it had, they effectively declared, suborned its fundamental commission from Christ to announce himself and his teaching to the whole world to the whims and fancies of those who wielded power in a lawless age, presumably in return for a relative form of peace or tolerated existence. Most of the Church's leadership in their own world, they were saying, had betrayed their founder and transferred their allegiance to power and money.

I sometimes joke that after more than a quarter of a century working on official Catholic newspapers and as part of the Church's not inconsiderable bureaucracy in Australia I've come to conclude that in a previous life I was probably a Viking, or perhaps one of the Mongol hordes sweeping west across the steppes into lush and fertile Europe. The reason, I explain, is that although I have no clear recollection of the details, I must have been burning down monasteries and destroying churches. Whatever I did was so spectacularly bad that the only suitable punishment was to be sent back in another life to work on a Catholic newspaper. After all, the single most disheartening aspect of my professional life for three decades now has been consistently reporting the reality of sexual abuse within official Catholic institutions. If the person to whom I'm talking doesn't get the joke I add 'In Australia'. If they still don't get it, I add: 'In the Twenty First Century'. Problems of the kind experienced by the bishops of Trosle have never been confined to just one period in the life of the Church.

Meanwhile, the experience of working in what is an unusual corner of journalism has led me to several conclusions. One is that the greatest and most important challenges and problems of the Church are not to be found in an age such as the present where indifference to Christianity and even official hostility to the Catholic Church are on the rise globally, including challenges that dismay Catholics and Christians in matters such as the basic right to practise their faith and to transmit it to their families. Until – very roughly – the middle of the twentieth century, Christians grew up and lived in a culture that displayed a generally socially positive acceptance of their faith's validity or was at least prepared to treat it and them with a certain basic respect. Within two or three generations people of Christian faith have transitioned to a world which has almost completely discarded, in affluent nations such as the US, Europe, Great Britain, Australia and New Zealand, its entire Christian spiritual, intellectual, cultural and social patrimony. Discarding the Christian tradition, except for public holidays and associated shopping seasons, has not been the end of the process of increasing global secularisation.

Following in its wake is an increasing cultural, legal and political assault against Christianity, including in cultures once regarded as its heartlands, and a rise in the hostility expressed towards both it and its adherents which is a truly revolutionary development in the history of the last 1500 years or more. That process has not been limited to the affluent American and western European cultures listed above. Central and Latin America, once overwhelmingly Catholic due to conquest by the Spanish and Portuguese, have also been secularised. There, the same phenomenon is occurring driven by largely the same factors evident elsewhere, including the rejection of the *ancien regime* which so strongly characterised the culture of Spanish Catholicism together with the contemporary revelations surrounding sexual abuse.

Meanwhile, that social and political hostility is increasingly expressed in authoritarian and totalitarian enactments by governments and authorities who reflect and express the sea-change described by Italian philosopher Augusto Del Noce as the global triumph of cultural Marxism from the 1960s onwards. Cultural Marxism is a phenomenon distinct from the primitive and genocidal doctrinaire Marxist-Leninist-Maoist expressions which rose to global power in the twentieth century but which collapsed at the conclusion of its eighth decade. Almost nowhere does anyone discuss concepts such as the proletariat, the dialectic and the necessity of the Revolution. Yet, as Del Noce argues, the Marxist philosophical methodology of analysing almost all issues as issues of privilege and oppression suppressing individuality, free will and autonomy appear to have triumphed everywhere – in the Academy, the public square, the media and in politics.

The entire world has changed. Christianity, which can be described as the informing spirit of Western civilisation for the last 1500 years in all its astonishing diversity (and with all its faults), has not simply fallen out of favour but has come to be viewed by the new elites who determine the key agendas of almost every aspect of the culture of modernity as its greatest threat, one which must be restricted, controlled and – ultimately – extirpated.

Despite a world utterly changed from anything it has even known, Christianity continues to proclaim its faith as the answer to the most important problems of human life. The contest for ideas and values in which it is presently engaged with what might be described as the anti-culture of modernity is epochal. It is no exaggeration to assert that the subsequent development and character of much of foreseeable history depends entirely on the outcome of this particular contest.

Yet, in such an argument for the heart of modernity, the Christian assertion must be scrutinised and tested against its own historical record if it is to have any credibility at all. Were that record one of universal and positive development wherever Christianity come to be accepted, the arguments – for Christians, at least, who are convinced that their faith is truly of divine origin and nature – would be much easier. But defending Christianity is not easy. In any debate involving Christianity's right to proclaim its faith or operate agencies and organisations inspired by and conforming to that faith, modernity is quick to point to Christianity's sins that apparently prove its claim to do good is hypocritical. Christian arguments for freedom of faith and maintenance of Christian institutions as well as the retention of legal and moral standards generated by the Judeo-Christian tradition are countered by gender ideologues, feminists, cultural Marxists and other critics arguing religion is merely a screen and a construct designed to retain an outdated institution's grip on power and dominance over individuals and society.

Eleven-hundred years after the bishops of Trosle condemned the corruption of their Church and society, contemporary events make secular critics' arguments more powerful. On 5 October 2020, French Catholic authorities made public a report that had been four years in the making and which, on the day of its release, generated headlines around the world. Commissioned by the French Catholic Bishops' Conference and the Conference of French Catholic Religious Orders, the 2500-page document had been painstakingly prepared by a 21-member interdisciplinary panel of experts from a wide range of religious backgrounds, none of whom were on the Church's payroll. Fronting the press conference making the report public was Jean-Marc Sauvé, a former French civil servant who led the panel known as the Independent Commission on Sexual Abuse in the Church (CIASE). The report's basic picture was shocking, yet tragically consistent and familiar in its general findings with other reports which have appeared in the last two decades. Significant among these reports are the 2004 John Jay College of Criminal Justice report into sexual abuse within the Catholic

Church in the US and the final findings of the Royal Commission into Institutional Responses to Child Sexual Abuse tabled in the Australian Parliament in December 2017.

Assuming that the French report's methodology and reporting remain unchallenged, the numbers contained in its pages were staggering and damning: from 1950 to 2020, the number of clerical victims of abuse in France was estimated to be about 216,000. Adding in abuse committed by Catholic Church employees, the estimated number rose to 330,000. Out of an estimated 115,000 priests who had served the Church in that period, somewhere between 2900 and 3200 were abusers. 'The Catholic Church is the place where the prevalence of sexual violence is at its highest, other than in family and friend circles' it said. The report also found children were more likely to be abused within Church settings than in state-run schools, holiday centres or camps. 'Faced with this scourge' the report concluded, 'for a very long time the Catholic Church's immediate reaction was to protect itself as an institution and it has shown complete, even cruel, indifference to those having suffered abuse'.

Dispensing with any discrete French civil service approach he may have acquired over the years, M. Sauvé was succinct to the point of bluntness. While most of the abuse uncovered by CIASE had occurred between 1950 and 1968, he revealed the abuse was systemic and not limited to 'a few black sheep that strayed from the flock'. More alarmingly, he suggested the abuse is still happening when admitting to reporters, 'The problem is not behind us, it is still there'.

The Report of the Independent Commission into sexual abuse within the French Catholic Church represents yet another hammer-blow falling on the credibility of the Catholic Church, given the generations of French bishops and religious leaders who either turned a blind eye to the problems as they surfaced or were criminally negligent in their duty to the most defenceless members of their flocks who, for generations, they had exhorted to be obedient to their authority. This disastrous state of affairs was also interpreted by critics of the Church as yet another damning vindication of their general cynicism regarding Christianity and, specifically, the Catholic Church. At one level, their reactions are difficult to argue with. Yet, at the same time, the report also represents a ray of hope, much like the bishops who met at Trosle. No problem, after all, can be solved, until it is confronted, named, and drawn out – kicking and screaming, if necessary – into clear daylight.

Christianity's critics, in addition to highlighting the shame of modern sexual abuse, are also right to highlight past sins of the Church. That history extends back to Judas Iscariot and his betrayal of Jesus Christ and to those who wanted the Messiah dead. While Christianity is uniquely responsible for the origins and evolution of Western civilisation, including saving much of our knowledge of the classical world from extinction throughout the Dark Ages, its entire story is one of both light and dark. The sins of Christians, or those who have identified themselves as Christians, have abounded at every turn of Christianity's development yet they have also redounded on the credibility of the Church. In fact, there is no stage of Christian history that is free of what might be called the sins of its members. Whether one points to the Hundred Years War, the viciousness of the Reformation conflicts, the practice of slavery for centuries by so-called Christian nations, the Spanish Inquisition, the harm wreaked upon indigenous peoples by their colonial 'Christian' conquerors, the truly shocking mass rape and murder of the sacking of Constantinople by the Fourth Crusade, the tragic recurring pogroms against Jews in 'Christian' European society and the phenomenon of anti-Semitism, the spectacular corruption of medieval and Renaissance popes – the list is endless and continues throughout the history of the Church.

One of the clearest formal acknowledgements of this historical reality came from Pope John Paul II – now St John Paul II – on 12 March 2000 when, as part of the celebration of the Great Year of Jubilee he had called to mark and celebrate two millennia of Christianity, he issued an apology for the sins of Christians throughout the history of the Church. The pope's decision to do so raised eyebrows in a number of places, not only within the corridors of the Vatican but further afield where some felt that perhaps the ageing pontiff was caving in a little too much to the growing currents of political correctness abroad in the world. Yet for John Paul II the matter was clear: Christians had sinned against others, against the most basic tenets of their faith and in a variety of ways throughout the existence of their Church and must ask for forgiveness, even if the request came relatively late in the historical day. The apology was, in the future saint's eyes, the culmination of his initiatives involving the Church's own 'examination of conscience' for the Jubilee Year. The-then pope's idea of a moment of atonement to acknowledge the sins, failings and shortcomings in the church's past was – aside from helping to heal historical wounds – also called to give Catholics a sense of reconciliation and make future evangelisation more credible.

'We forgive and we ask forgiveness!' he said during a unique Lenten liturgy in St Peter's Basilica where he and other top Church leaders issued a 'request for pardon'. The sins enumerated by John Paul II and other church officials included those against Christian unity, the use of violence in serving the truth, hostility toward Jews and other religions [and] the marginalisation of women… among others. Abuse was not specifically named, if only for the reason that the Church, including John Paul II, was still coming to grips with the actual extent and fullness of its destruction. The devastating coverage of the *Boston Globe*'s investigation of the Archdiocese of Boston was still two years away from publication. Meanwhile, John Paul II said, while the church has had many saints, the truth was that some of its members have also shown disobedience to God and inconsistency with the faith – in the past and present. Historians may well debate whether the precise truth is closer to 'some' or 'many', but the pope's admission was important as too many Christians, caught in the culture wars of the present, make the mistake of defensively romanticising Christianity. Interestingly, the word used by John Paul II to describe one of the effects of the sins of Christians on the Church itself was 'disfigurement', calling to mind the image of the face of Christ disfigured by the blows suffered during his own Passion. When Christians have sinned against others, he seemed to be saying, the effects of their actions and words do not stop with the victims, but actually contribute to distorting the true nature of the Church and its faith in the eyes of those who suffer and all those who witness such crimes. When Christians sin against others, in other words, they also sin against the Church, they sin against the truth and they sin against Christ.

Also apologising for past Catholic intolerance was then-Cardinal Joseph Ratzinger (also the future Pope Benedict XVI) in his role as prefect of the Congregation for the Doctrine of the Faith; a body created nearly 500 years earlier and formally known as the Supreme Sacred Congregation of the Roman and Universal Inquisition. 'Even men of the church, in the name of faith and morals', Cardinal Ratzinger admitted, 'have sometimes used methods not in keeping with the Gospel in the solemn duty of defending the truth'. One such example, out of many that have occurred, saw Church authorities hanging and burning the fiery Dominican friar Girolamo Savanorola in 1498, together with two of his Dominican brethren, for what today would be considered merely highly eccentric views about the Church. It was also Cardinal Ratzinger, one of the Church's most gifted teachers of the faith in centuries, who, as Pope John Paul II lay dying in the Vatican in 2005 shocked the world when he not only publicly confirmed and named the abuse phenomenon for what it is but pointed directly at who was responsible. 'How much filth there is in the Church, and even among those who, in the priesthood, ought to belong entirely to him! How much pride, how much self-complacency!' he prayed publicly at the ninth station commemorating Jesus falling for the third time under the weight of his cross.

The sins of Christians may seem to onlookers as confirmation that Christianity, whatever the positives it may have contributed to human existence over two thousand years or so, is ultimately empty – proof that it may raise some interesting questions and even represent certain positive values and historical achievements, but is merely just another human attempt to make sense of the universe and life that ultimately fails when it is lived out. Yet the understandable conclusion that because Christians are sinners Christianity must also be false fails to comprehend Christianity's understanding of the nature of sin and the problems it represents for all human lives. And it is also a failure of logic. Because I may be mugged in the street by a drunk Irishman does not mean that I need to fear the entire Irish nation whenever I go out for a walk and would offer zero justification for enacting universal anti-Irish laws and statutes. Yet it is also true the sins of Christians have an added and more devastating consequence and significance. Because the Church portrays itself and its faith as the answer to eternal questions about what constitutes ethical and moral behaviour based on the explicit teachings of its founder, the sins of Christians seem far worse and far more hypocritical and therefore more discrediting to the wider public.

What those condemning Christianity fail to realise is that to be human is to suffer temptation and be prone to sin. God created man with free will and as a result many Christians and many in the Church are guilty of denying Christ's teachings and committing evil. As detailed in the Book of Genesis, this tendency towards evil is inherited from the very first human beings, our parents, who, despite being in an intimate personal relationship with God, chose their own desires above the commands of their divine creator. As a result both were expelled from paradise – the Garden of Eden – and humanity has consequently been subject to suffering: death, pain, betrayal, sickness and all the other evils that are as much the story of human history as is its achievements and triumphs. Just as we inherit red hair or blue eyes from our parents, intrinsically flawed human nature can only beget children who carry their parents' spiritual DNA as well. This mystery is what the Church describes as the *mysterium iniquitatis*. How is it that we can – and do – choose what we know to be destructive to ourselves and to others? The mystery of evil, meanwhile, is present in every human being, from the greatest pope to the lowest thief. It can only be overcome by the power of Christ, who invites us to share our lives with his.

It is this reality that famously saw Pope Francis describe the Church as a field hospital for sinners in an interview in 2013, an image which resonated with many, Catholic and otherwise, in an age where the Church has been humiliated and discredited by the worst of all possible crimes having been uncovered within its own ranks. The sad and sorry tale of the demise of Mr Ted McCarrick, once known as Cardinal Theodore McCarrick, the former 'king-maker' of the Catholic Church in the US and a confident of popes (including John Paul II, Benedict XVI and Francis), showed everyone how deep the rot had entered as it was revealed that for decades the former cardinal had routinely hunted out seminarians to sleep in his bed and used his exceptional rank and authority in the Church to derail questions, investigations and allegations. Despite credible allegations of abuse of children, including a boy he had baptised, Church authorities did nothing to hinder his stellar career or the significant influence he exercised over key appointments in the Church throughout the US.

In the early decades of the twenty-first century, the Church has entered a landscape utterly changed from the milieu with which it has been familiar for centuries. While it has experienced opposition, resistance and persecutions throughout its history, the titanic clash of the values of the Gospel with the anti-culture of modernity seem to have all been going in favour of modernity. Throughout the affluent world, in particular, the Judeo-Christian basis of moral and social order has largely been dumped. The problem with the new state of social organisation which is theoretically based on ensuring maximum personal autonomy is that it appears increasingly authoritarian and totalitarian with regard to anyone who does not accept the *diktats* of the state or its elites.

In countries such as Australia and elsewhere, successive generations of the young have found the moral relativism, the nihilism and scientific certainty of modernity's secularist project apparently too persuasive. Participation in the celebration of the Eucharist, for Catholics the heart of the Christian life, has plummeted as vast numbers of Catholics have effectively exited the Church and rejected its most important teachings about the human person, human life and God. The Church itself is riven internally by a fault line which can be described as that separating a hermeneutic of discontinuity from a hermeneutic of continuity. The former asserts that Christianity needs to conform itself to the values and teachings of the age in order to remain relevant. The latter interprets the Church beginning with Christ and his teaching, its faith and its tradition, accepting that what God wills in matters such as marriage or the sanctity of human life, for example, cannot be changed at whim by humanity to suit its own preferences or fashionable trends.

In 1958, three years before the commencement of the landmark event in the life of the modern Church known as Vatican II, the young German theology Professor Joseph Ratzinger gave a lecture entitled *The New Pagans and the Church*. In the talk, Ratzinger surveyed the new reality dawning on the Church in its supposed heartland of European culture. Ratzinger acknowledged that Europe was regarded as synonymous with Christian culture but flatly rejected the truth of that assertion.

This so-called Christian Europe for almost four hundred years has become the birthplace of a new paganism, which is growing steadily in the heart of the Church, and threatens to undermine her from within... The outward shape of the modern Church is determined essentially by the fact that, in a totally new way, she has become the Church of pagans, and is constantly becoming even more so. She is no longer, as she once was, a Church composed of pagans who have become Christians, but a Church of pagans, who still call themselves Christians, but actually have become pagans.

The resonances between the bishops of Trosle a millennium earlier and the young, gifted theology professor are impossible to ignore. At this distance, and considering Fr Ratzinger was speaking a year before Pope (now Saint) John XXIII announced his decision to convoke the defining moment in the life of the modern Church, Vatican II, his remarks seem uncannily prescient. They dovetail neatly with his comparatively better-known comments given in a 1969 radio broadcast in his native Germany where he predicted that the Church of the future would lose much of its power, its possessions – and its numbers. Nevertheless, he said, a Church sifted by the onslaught of modernity would, while being far, far smaller in number, also be more faithful, purer, a Church of a living and authentic faith rather than an ossified institution weak to penetration by the ultimate mediocrities: corruption due to love of power and money. While it is undeniable Christians have sinned against many others in the two-thousand-year history of their Church, it may yet be observed at some distant point in the future that the greatest sin of the Christians of our time was that the overwhelming majority simply did not live their faith.

Peter Rosengren is a media and communications specialist with a long history in journalism and publishing. Currently he is the editor of the Sydney-based The Catholic Weekly.

CHRISTIANITY: THE WAY FORWARD

TESS LIVINGSTONE

For Christians daunted about the best way forward, the most reassuring words are surely those of Christ near the end of Matthew's Gospel (Mt 28:20): 'All authority in heaven and on earth has been given to me. Go therefore and make disciples of all nations, baptising them in the name of the Father and of the Son and of the Holy Spirit, and teaching them to obey everything that I have commanded you. And remember, I am with you always to the end of the age'.

Twenty centuries on from founding His Church at Caesarea Philippi, now known as Kesariya, in northern Israel, nothing less than His Divine guidance could have ensured Christianity's survival through persecutions, schisms, martyrdoms and the imprisonment of some of its finest sons and daughters. That Divine guidance is also clear in the saintliness, heroism and suprahuman generosity that is part of the Christian story. And provided atonement is made for grave sins, it is Divine guidance that will bring the faithful through the appalling scandal of child sexual abuse and coverups.

This chapter will focus heavily on two profoundly important developments unfolding in the third decade of the Church's twenty-first century. They deserve attention because how they are resolved will determine Christianity's future. One development concerns the Church's relationship with the world, especially with China, as that nation pursues its quest to dominate the Indo-Pacific and further afield. The second development concerns the Church's understanding of its own raison d'etre and its relationship with God, especially as expressed in the Eucharist, described in the Catholic Catechism as the 'source and summit' of Christian life. Related issues include the crisis of belief and confusion rife within the Church's own ranks and Christianity's role in the public square. God's tendency to write straight in crooked lines, as St Teresa of Avila (1515–1582) described it, makes venturing an opinion on the way forward problematic and speculative. Our best hope, as St Augustine said in the fourth century and St Ignatius Loyola said in the sixteenth century is to: 'Pray as though everything depended on God. Work as though everything depended on you'.

Early in his Pontificate, Pope Francis announced that Christians were not living in 'an era of change' but in a 'change of era'. This quickly became evident when speakers such as US population and pro-abortion advocate Jeffrey Sachs and other green-Left radicals became fixtures at Vatican conferences. In late 2021, Francis appointed Sachs to the Pontifical Academy of Social Sciences. The Pope has never hidden his ambition to remake the Church. 'There is no need to create another church, but to create a different church,' he said in October 2021, at the opening of a two-year synod on the subject of 'synodality'. It will involve two years of meetings, in the Vatican and around the worldon the subject of future meetings (synods). It will conclude in October 2023 – with a synod of bishops in Rome. It won't be cheap. It is also highly debatable and remains to be seen whether endless 'dialogue' and endless cups of potent café Italiano add to the sum total of the faith. Pope Benedict, in his days as an academic, was sceptical about 'committee Catholicism' and a German synod. In 1970 he said the faithful rightly become indifferent to 'the church apparatus talking about itself'. In the end, he said, people 'don't want to go on hearing more about how priests and high-ranking Catholics do their jobs, but what God wants from them in life and death and what he does not want'.

Beyond the talkfest, which coincides with similar undertakings in various countries, including Australia, Francis's determination to link Christianity to a particular ideology is clear. His 2015 green encyclical, Laudato Si, for example, was quasi-Marxist in parts, calling for 'enforceable international agreements' and 'international institutions… empowered to impose sanctions', not only for greenhouse emissions and other environmental damage but also to eliminate poverty.

Far more seriously, amid growing geostrategic instability, especially in the Indo-Pacific region, the Vatican, regrettably, has invested its moral authority on the wrong side of history. Its 2018 secret pact with the Chinese Communist government of Xi Jinping, renewed in 2020, has never been made public. But it handed Communist officials significant control over the appointment of bishops. In that respect, it went further than the shameful Reichskonkordat of July 1933, between the Vatican and the newly formed Nazi government of Germany. It is a worse deal, incredibly, with yet another dictator. Hong Kong Cardinal Joseph Zen, a prophetic figure of the twenty-first century church in professing the church's core mission in a hostile environment, recognised the dangers from the outset. Concerned about the safety of underground Churchgoers and clergy, who had stuck with Rome through decades of torture and coercion from CCP authorities, Cardinal Zen recognised the pact as a 'betrayal… giving the flock into the mouths of the wolves'.

Cardinal Zen feared a repeat of the unprincipled Ospolitik (German for eastern politics) of the 1960s, when the Vatican appeased the Soviet Union by abandoning ardent anti-Communists such as Hungarian Cardinal Joseph Mindszenty. After being tortured and imprisoned following a show trial, Mindszenty took refuge in the US embassy in Budapest for 15 years. In the early stages of détente, however, the Vatican ordered him, against his will, to leave Hungary.

After the first agreement with China in 2018, Vatican-based

Argentinian Bishop Sanchez Sorondo made the ludicrous claim the Chinese state exemplified Catholic social justice teaching. In practice, the agreement did not bring Chinese Christians the freedoms that many, naively, had hoped. On the contrary, China stepped up persecution of most religions. It imposed strict new rules, requiring clergy to promote the values of the Chinese Communist Party. Under Xi Jinping's 'sinicisation of religion' diktat, Christian churches are under pressure, with religious signage and imagery destroyed or replaced – Mao instead of the Virgin Mary; Xi instead of Jesus.

When Cardinal Zen, 89, visited Rome in 2020 to plead with Francis not to renew the agreement, the pope snubbed him, refusing him an audience. From there the situation deteriorated. In August 2021, police arrested an underground priest, Father Liu Maochun, from the diocese of Mindong, near Shanghai, and tortured him when he refused to join the state-sanctioned Independent Church, part of the pro-Communist Party Patriotic Association. 'After 10 hours of torture, six policemen took him by the hand and forced him to sign,' Christian newsagency asianews.it reported. Ten priests and 10 trainee priests recently spent nine weeks in detention.

The absurdity of the Vatican's position was crystallised in September 2021. Despite China's militarisation of the South China Sea, which it claims illegally, its ruthless crushing of Hong Kong's democracy, its $20 billion trade war against Australia, incursions into Japanese airspace and its determination to over-run Taiwan, the Vatican Secretary of State, Italian Cardinal Pietro Parolin, objected to the US-UK-Australia security pact, AUKUS, under which Australia will buy eight-nuclear powered submarines. As Paul Kelly wrote in *The Australian* in October 2021: 'This debate is going to affect Australian Catholics. The conflict between the Vatican's view of China and Australia's view of China will only intensify. It is a conflict between the Vatican view of the Catholic interest and the secular Australian view of the national interest. But there is another conclusion – Australian Catholics shouldn't follow the Pope on China'.

The Vatican's attitude is also deeply disturbing to other nations in the region, including the Philippines, whose population of 110 million is predominantly Catholic. Despite the Philippines being vindicated when it took China to the International Court of Justice in 2016, China continues its military build-up in the South China Sea, on islands it does not own.

Apologists for the secret Vatican-China pact pretend it brought the work of previous popes St John Paul II and Benedict XVI to fruition. Both wanted progress with China. But neither would entertain the compromises the pact entails. Only a change of direction during a future Pontificate will salvage the Church's credibility on the issue. St John Paul II, like Francis, was also heavily engaged in international politics. His efforts, however, were directed against Soviet Communism, the Church's long time, implacable enemy.

Religious persecutions like those inflicted on the underground church in China since 1949 are nothing new. In the Anglo-Irish world, two come to mind. The first are the Mass rocks of Ireland, where the 'golden priests' with their wooden chalices celebrated Masses in secret in the penal years, from 1695 to 1829. The rocks were often in secluded glades, on hills with sweeping views of surrounding countryside and any soldiers or spies on the prowl. One Mass rock, preserved in the backblocks of County Limerick, overlooks the Golden Vale. Visiting it feels like an elixir for the soul, like the icy spring water that cascades down the nearby hill.

Another inspiring testament to faith is a large farmhouse, deep in the Oxfordshire countryside in England, Lyford Grange. Driving there one unforgettable winter afternoon a few years ago, the silent fields and unmarked lanes seemed interminable. In the sixteenth century, on horseback, it must have felt like the ends of the earth. Back then, as on

11 September 2001, fanatical religious hatred can be a deadly motivator. Despite Lyford Grange's remoteness and its well-concealed priest holes, St Edmund Campion, an Oxford-educated Jesuit, was captured there in July 1581, during the reign of Elizabeth I. His crime was offering Mass and preaching. Taken to London, he was convicted of high treason, tortured in the Tower of London for five months, then dragged through the streets behind a cart to the Tyburn gallows, near the present Marble Arch, where he was hanged, drawn and quartered.

Far from being unique to the savagery of centuries past, more people died for the Christian faith in the twentieth century than in the preceding 19 centuries combined. Some are famous, such as St Maximilian Kolbe and St Teresa Benedicta of the Cross (Edith Stein), who were all martyred under the Nazis in World War II. Millions more died in the Soviet gulags and in China under Mao.

The future of Catholicism and Christian belief hinges on an enormous battle over the Catholic Mass currently unfolding. It is being driven, however, not by the Church's external enemies but from the highest echelons within its own ranks. Battlelines are drawn for a long, intense struggle. It may be resolved during the next Pontificate; it may take far longer.

Within Catholicism, Christianity's largest body, there is a struggle between tradition and innovation, between continuity with the past and rupture with the past. The struggle focuses on how the policies of the Second Vatican Council should be applied and interpreted. It centres on the Catholic Mass and the beliefs underpinning it.

On 16 July 2021, Francis, backed by senior curial players, moved to crush centuries of tradition in an instruction entitled, ironically, Traditionis Custodes (Custodians of Tradition). Traditional Latin Masses were 'not to take place any longer' in normal parishes, the apostolic letter specified. No new Latin Mass groups were to be established. Bishops were given sweeping power to decide whether to allow any Latin Masses in their dioceses and if so, when and where they were to be said and by which priests – but not in normal parishes. The instruction is revolutionary.

The traditional Mass, which evolved from the early centuries onwards, and was largely unchanged for 1500 years until the Second Vatican Council (1962–1965) has been earmarked to be strangled, the sooner the better according to supporters of Traditionis Custodes. As recently as 2007, Pope Benedict had affirmed the right of all priests to say Mass using the traditional rite, without the permission of bishops. The traditional rite was never abrogated by Vatican II, Benedict confirmed. It remained intact through 'immemorial custom'. And in *Quo Primum* in 1570, Pope Pius V stated that the traditional Mass must stand for all time, and that anyone who dared to violate that perpetual permission would 'incur the wrath of almighty God'.

Traditionis Custodes is about far more than the Latin language. The post-Vatican II Mass, after all, can also be said in Latin, which is the Church's official language. The crackdown is about the theology of the traditional Mass, which invokes a powerful sense of the transcendent and the supernatural, the 'otherness' of God. The New Rite is more egalitarian and communal. Only 13 per cent of the prayers in the old Missal found their way unchanged into the post-Vatican II Missal. More than half were discarded, and the remainder were substantially edited according to research by liturgical scholars. In declaring that only the post-Second Vatican Council liturgical books were the 'unique expression of the lex orandi (the law) of the Roman rite'– and therefore a reflection of what Christians believe – Francis discarded centuries of belief and tradition under which the old Mass emerged. Writing in 1855, English scholar St John Henry Newman noted that the Traditional Latin Mass 'is virtually unchanged since the third century'. In 1912, British scholar Adrian Fortescue noted that 'from roughly the time of St. Gregory (540–604) we have the text of the Mass, its order and arrangement, as a sacred tradition that no one ventured to touch except in unimportant details'.

On careful reading, Pope Francis's declaration that only the New Rite is the 'unique expression of the lex orandi (the law of prayer that shapes belief) of the Roman rite' raises a profound and perplexing issue. If the Old Rite was the 'unique expression of the lex orandi of the Roman Rite' for centuries until the 1970s, which it was, what has changed? Why such a rupture? Are we now in a different Church, with a different faith, with roots dating back only to 1965? In so far as it has ruptured the continuity that prevailed over 20 centuries, Traditionis Custodes is profoundly disturbing to many who attend both forms of the Mass.

One of the ironies of the current situation is that in recent decades, after St John Paul II opened the door to its revival with the publication of Ecclesia Dei (God's Church) in 1988, the Old Mass has rapidly emerged as one of the few growth areas of Christianity in the West, especially among young people and families. As the Ignatius Press introduction to the Old Mass states: 'This sacrifice offered by Christ alone, was perfect and no other could add to it, but it is Christ's wish that we who are members of His mystical body should be able to take part in this Sacrifice and make our own offering of it to the Father. And so we join our self-offering to Christ's; this is what we do in the Mass'.

Many Catholics alternate between both forms, often noticing the strong sense of the Sacred the Old Rite imparts. That Rite is also attracting strong numbers of converts and vocations. In 2018, Britain's *Catholic Herald* reported that 20 per cent of the 114 men ordained to the priesthood in France that year had studied at seminaries dedicated to the traditional Mass.

It was probably no coincidence that the weeks leading up Francis's instruction brought an unprecedented crackdown in St Peter's Basilica, the Mother Church of Christianity, on both the traditional Latin Mass and the post-Vatican II Mass. Priests were barred from saying either Mass, individually, at the Basilica's many side altars, which had been a hive of activity for centuries. Under the new rules, individual Masses were to be replaced with several larger, concelebrated Masses each day. By their nature, these put a greater emphasis on the 'community meal' aspect of the liturgy rather than the recreation of Christ's Sacrifice on Calvary.

German Cardinal Gerhard Muller, the former prefect of the Congregation for the Doctrine of the Faith who was sacked by Francis, said the order banning individual Masses at the side altars of St Peter's was a 'merciless, authoritarian document, imposed without consultation' (in a church in which synods and consultation are supposedly a priority). The move disregarded 'the Catholic spiritual tradition of the priesthood to celebrate the Mass every day' and was proof of the 'self-secularisation of the church', Cardinal Muller said.

Even in more liberal dioceses, Traditionis Custodes has not been well received. It provokes arguments most bishops do not want to have; many, sensibly, turn a blind eye to the healthy numbers attending traditional Masses in their dioceses. And in a positive development in February 2022, Pope Francis himself granted all members of the Fraternity of Saint Peter permission to continue to offer the Sacrifice of the Mass and celebrate all Sacraments in the traditional rite in their own churches and oratories, or in other churches with the permission of local bishops. The Fraternity was established for that purpose in 1988. It has 300 priests and 150 seminarians from 30 countries and serves in more than 130 dioceses in five continents, including Australia.

At the opposite end of the liturgical spectrum, the other growth area of Christianity, especially in the US but also in Australia, is Pentecostal Protestantism. The World Population Review shows Christianity is the religion of 2.4 billion people, who worship in hundreds of denominations. The Catholic Church, with 1.2 billion members, is the largest. Pentecostal and evangelical churches, while still relatively small, now have about 644 million followers, including about 500,000 in Australia. Their schools, often built in outer suburban and regional areas where parents are eager for a wider choice and better-quality education with strong, Gospel-based values, are increasingly in demand.

Schools are also one of the Catholic Church's strengths. They educate about one in five Australian students, from kindergarten to Year 12. The church's involvement in tertiary education is also gaining traction, through the Australian Catholic University, Notre Dame University and Campion College, a privately funded liberal arts centre of excellence near Parramatta. Regardless of the educational merits of Catholic schools, many parents and clergy despair of the low Mass attendance rates among the young people emerging from them.

The latest available national Mass attendance report, from 2016, showed an attendance rate of 11.8 per cent of Catholics, about 623,400 people each weekend. Of those, a third were aged 60–74, with the highest attendance among those 70 and older. Among young adult Catholics aged 20–34, less than six per cent attend Mass on a typical weekend. The figures are indicative of a serious crisis of faith. The causes of that crisis – including poor religious instruction in the 1970s and 1980s which undermined the commitment of the generation who are today's Catholic parents and teachers – are not easily overcome.

Nor have Christian schools been spared the malaise in humanities teaching that has afflicted much of Australia's education system. Education Minister Alan Tudge's dismay at curriculum writers almost erasing Christianity from the curriculum is important. Christian schools of all denominations should be in the forefront of redressing the trend. Sydney's Catholic Archbishop, Anthony Fisher, set out key issues facing Christianity when he told the Church's Plenary Council in October 2021:

*Wake up Catholic Australia! There's a bushfire consuming faith
in this land. Disillusionment over child sexual abuse has accelerated
the secularisation of recent decades. Many now identify with no
particular religion, institutional identity has corroded, young people
are inoculated to faith by the culture, and some churchgoers are out
of sorts with Catholic teaching. This Council must consider how
we'll proclaim the Gospel of Jesus Christ to those without faith, those
needing more formation and those yet to embrace their true identity
as missionary disciples.*

He set out the challenge of non-practising Catholics:

*Wake up to the flood of non-practice! Entire demographics
are missing. Too few now take part in Mass and Reconciliation.
Volunteers and resources are thin on the ground. Family, parish
and school are all under stress when we need them most. With the
flood-alarm of disengagement sounding, we need common pastoral
action to rekindle enthusiasm and inspire active participation in the
Eucharistic community.*

An accomplished moral theologian, he also urged Synod participants to:

*Wake up to the pandemic of moral confusion. Judeo-Christian
influence on law and culture has waned, conscience rights are
threatened, and people of faith driven from the public square. Just
lately Australia has adopted some of the world's most extreme
abortion, euthanasia, marriage and sexuality laws... Our Council
must drive new adventures in preaching the Gospel of Life and Love,
Justice and Mercy, in unpacking Catholic morality for the faithful,
and in being voices and servants of 'the little ones'.*

Archbishop Fisher also underlined the vocational crisis in the
Catholic community:

*Wake up: the vocational grounding of the Church is shaking.
Sacramental marriage is in free fall and marriages failing. Religious*

are an endangered species. Good Shepherdly priests are sorely needed
to provide sacraments, pastoral leadership and evangelisation. We
look to this Council for new approaches to promoting, discerning and
forming people for these crucial vocations, as well as the baptismal
vocation in the world, to strengthening Christian identity and
sustaining mission.

He concluded with a message of hope: 'Alert to what should alarm us, but confident in God's grace, we can respond to the signs of our times – with intelligence and humility, patience and hope, compassion and fidelity'.

For all its human weaknesses, examples abound in many cultures of Christianity persevering against the odds. At times when the world has seemed to be at rock bottom the church has brought forward spiritual leaders who have helped transform the spiritual and earthly lives of millions. St Benedict (480–547), the founder of Western Monasticism; St Vincent de Paul (1581–1660); St Mary of the Cross MacKillop (1842–1909), St Teresa of Calcutta (1910–1997) and Eileen O'Connor (1892–1921), founder of Our Lady's Nurses for the Poor in Sydney, are prime examples, among many. Christianity could do with a few real leaders now, to read the signs of our own times. If the pattern of previous centuries holds they will emerge.

Archbishop Fisher, deeply concerned about the battle to legalise euthanasia in NSW, recently sought the intercession of Eileen O'Connor against the legislation. O'Connor, who is on the path to canonisation, lived most of her 28 years with a serious spinal injury. She was dwarfed, often immobile and always in pain. These days, in some people's eyes, she would be a candidate for 'voluntary assisted dying'. She and her nurses helped countless Australians in desperate need. Euthanasia, the Archbishop said, is the 'very antithesis of Eileen's caring for people to the end'.

At micro level, parish and family traditions make a difference. Australia's 2016 Mass survey found attendance rates of people born in non-English-speaking countries had remained stable (about 23 per cent) since 1996, while attendance among those born in Australia has declined, from 17 per cent in 1996 to nine per cent in 2016. Educators cannot ignore the problem for another generation.

Significant efforts to improve faith education have been under way since the mid-1990s. But better textbooks alone are not enough, according to retired Melbourne auxiliary bishop Peter Elliott, editor of the outstanding *To Know Worship and Love* texts widely used in Catholic schools. As with other subjects, much depends on the knowledge and attitudes of teachers and parents. Bishop Elliott believes Parish Priests need to spend more time in staffrooms and classrooms and take advantage of opportunities such as First Communion and Confirmation to draw parents into adult catechetical education. In many parishes, one of the most distressing aspects of ministry is to see full churches (rightly so) for such vital Sacramental celebrations, but with almost all the families missing in subsequent weeks.

The public square is increasingly important for Christian leaders, whose responsibility, to paraphrase Augustine, is to live in both the City of God and the City of Man. Radical secularists want the voices of Christianity silenced. But these voices are more important than ever, with lawmakers in almost every state rushing headlong into what has proved a slippery slope in Europe and North America– Euthanasia. Abortion laws around Australia are now so liberal (indeed callous) that a small number of late-term aborted children who survive the procedure are left to die, without medical intervention. The Queensland Parliament heard in 2016 that the previous year, 27 aborted babies of five months gestation survived, only to later die after not receiving treatment. 'Once a decision to terminate is made, that is the outcome in accordance with the family's wishes', a Queensland Health spokesperson said.

At the most grassroots level of all, one Friday in October 2021, I returned to the parish where I grew up, to attend Mass on my Mum's anniversary. Half a century ago, at primary school, Friday mornings always included First Friday Mass or Benediction. Every child was familiar with St John's account of the Crucifixion (the Gospel read on First Fridays) and with the powerful Benediction hymns about the Real Presence of Christ. Decades later I learned these were written by St Thomas Aquinas (1225-1274). There were worse ways to form children in the faith.

These days, one of my friends in the parish helps out with the school children. She was there that morning – to teach the pre-schoolers the Sign of the Cross! It's a start, on what needs to be a long road back.

Tess Livingstone is the chief leader writer of The Australian *and* The Weekend Australian. *She is the biographer of Cardinal George Pell and the author or editor of a dozen other books on theology, business and children's literature.*